Brian O.

With your
recent m&A (Yan?)
activity — now is the
time to put the
right processes and
structure in place
find sustainable
Xcellence!

Leadership
XCELLENCE

Leadership
XCELLENCE

The Heart of Leadership
Is Not Business, It's Personal

KEITH THURGOOD, PHD
MAJOR GENERAL (RET), USA

Leadership Xcellence: The Heart of Leadership Is Not Business, It's Personal
By Keith Thurgood, PhD, Major General (Ret), USA

Business & Economics : Leadership

ISBN (paperback) 978-1-0879-2418-2

Edited by Tamma Ford
Proofreading by Jeffrey Cleek
Book design by DTPerfect.com

"We exist temporarily through what we take, but we live forever through what we give."

—Douglas Lawson

Leadership is a personal journey of Xcellence. My own story is one that reflects the impact of hundreds of exceptional people who have touched my life. In many ways I am a composite of what they have taught me. One of the things I have learned in my journey is that the character of the leader determines performance, and that leadership is about *being* and not just about *doing*. Leaders Learn, DO and BEcome better when they understand that leadership is first and foremost personal. It is about finding your voice and then helping others find theirs. It is about being crystal clear about your purpose. It is about seeing others, not as they are, but what they too can become.

The measure of one's life is not only reflected in what has been harvested, but what has been planted. We are all either takers or givers; multipliers or diminishers; authentic or artificial. The choice is ours.

≈

Thanks Mom and Dad for showing me the way. Thank you Carol for keeping the home fires burning and sticking with me. Thanks to Heather, Aaron, Ryan, Lindsey and Trever…and all 15 of my grandchildren…the treasures of my life. Make a difference and leave a legacy as you step along your leadership journey.

Contents

Challenges and Opportunities

In any leadership role, you enter a world where you are presented with a set of challenges and opportunities.

Surprisingly, the initial challenges are not about operations or change management. The first challenge is really about change leadership, starting with you. Being a self-aware leader is a critical first step on your leadership journey. It begins with getting to know yourself. Being honest about your personal leadership attributes and characteristics and understanding where you are right now juxtaposed against the kind of leader you want to be, is the perfect starting place for your leadership development journey. Being honest about the type of person you are in this moment and the type of person you want to become is a difficult and often daunting task requiring honest self-reflection and a degree of personal tenacity. Being a self-aware leader positions you to develop and improve your own competencies while opening the door to influencing others.

The challenge of change leadership is recognizing that you are not the biggest, brightest and smartest person in the room. It requires putting aside your ego so others can grow and develop into effective leaders, which in turn allows you to build high-performing teams built on trust. As a servant leader, you start to realize that the focus is not on "me" or the next senior-level role or promotion. You understand that failure is a tutor, not a tragedy, and that the pursuit of excellence is a journey. You recognize your own warts and commit to positive change.

The challenge of change leadership is to be grounded and centered on deeply personal values that drive your behavior. Great leaders walk their talk, and their lives reflect consistency and congruency. Their behavior reflects deeply held beliefs and aligns with a personal vision as well as the values, vision, and mission of the organization to which they belong.

Finally, the challenge of change leadership is to become a trustworthy person…this is the heart of effective leadership. These leaders model the right behaviors and develop a leadership pipeline. These leaders keep the promises they make to themselves and to others.

Leadership opportunities are numerous and important. Effective leadership allows you to identify and build on your strengths. You also have the chance to identify and guide your team members so they too can build on their strengths. Going from strength to strength helps the organization achieve and sustain excellence.

The opportunities of leadership imply continuous learning and growing—becoming better and always being willing to improve. Those you lead will follow your example and find ways to expand their know-how and skill sets as well. In that way, the entire team builds on their strengths. As the team builds on their strengths, there is a cascading and compounding effect on the individual and team. Not only am I demonstrating trust, which is the glue needed to develop teams and sustain high performance, but I am also setting the stage for continued growth and development. Indeed, filling the leadership pipeline is one of my primary responsibilities as an effective leader that influences others with a purpose.

The opportunities of leadership involve influence. This is not like political pull where there is manipulation or fact-spinning. This is where your values, behaviors, attitudes and character speak so loudly that your followers pattern their lives after yours—meaning they imitate the right behaviors that build trust, confidence and influence. As a leader of influence, your team receives encouragement from you.

Great leaders walk their talk, and their lives reflect consistency and congruency.

You are not only interested in the results or what you harvest, but you are also deeply involved in what is being planted. Your actions and words motivate them to strive for excellence and take risks while recognizing that failure is a teacher, not a tragedy. They are willing to do this because they trust you to do the right thing and that you will act consistently… you will give them the right tools and resources and provide top cover when needed. They become creative and empowered problem solvers. They have a "solve for yes" mindset focused on results and outcomes. The opportunity of leadership is to develop a fully engaged team that is passionate, energized and driven by purpose.

Every year, there are a plethora of new books about leadership. I'll be the first to recognize the world probably doesn't need another. But my hope is that this book will be useful to you specifically. By sharing the lessons I've learned as I continue to grow and become a more effective leader, I hope you will gain more insight in your personal journey. I hope this will be a tool that provides the right direction and azimuth regardless of where you are today. Whether you are:

- A student or recent hire who hasn't been able to test your leadership wings in situ—but desire to get as much right as possible as early as possible.
- A seasoned leader who has too often witnessed the disengagement of your team or has never quite achieved full engagement at any time.
- A leader who recognizes the problem is not in the team or "out there", but right here, with you, right now.
- A leader who faces the challenges of change management and change leadership and is looking in the mirror wondering what the solution could possibly be.
- A leader who is charged with developing the next generation of leaders and needs a place to begin.
- An individual who simply finds persistent dissatisfaction in their workplace performance.

I have been in each of those positions, so I know you can study leadership books all you want and still see no progress. Yes, you'll get a few nuggets here and there. Leadership, however, is experiential...that is why we call it "leadership development." You cannot just read and magically be that great leader everyone is happy to follow. You have to focus on the kind of leader you want to be first. Some mistakes will be made along the way...that is part of the development journey. Mistakes and opportunities call for analysis and correction. Get mad if you need to, but then get over it and move on. To make significant progress you must be willing to make changes and move forward on your personal path to "becoming" a great leader. Yes, leadership is about influence and bringing others along with you, but you will discover, as I did, that the heart of great leadership is not necessarily about activity. It is about "becoming" the kind of leader that you know you should be. Leadership is not business. It's personal.

PART ONE

The Heart of Leadership

*To Lead: / verb /. From Old English for 'to guide', 'to travel';
from the 13th century for 'to be in the first place'.*

Immediately, we think of "taking someone somewhere", "taking or guiding or directing others in a predetermined new direction". Both images imply doing something with a specific purpose in mind.

Leading implies having control and taking charge—by going out in front of your troops, your team and organization, or your family. Leading is about showing the way, directing, and influencing people to want to do what you want them to do. These images imply that there are followers.

But why would anyone want to follow you anyway? Part of the answer lies in you…the leader. To articulate a vision and noble purpose that inspires and motivates others is one reason why others might follow you. But, to sustain long-term influence, the real question is not about what you do, but who you are. That is the heart of the matter. It begs questions like these: What kind of leader should you be, so your example is compelling and influential enough for others to follow and achieve great things? Are you that person today? How do you close the personal gap between who you are today and who you can become tomorrow? Those are a few of the questions I answer in the first part of the book.

1

At the Heart of Great Leadership

My working life has been rich in experiences for me, especially in so many positions throughout my career which have served to shape my thinking and development as a leader. My leadership career started with my experiences as a newly commissioned officer in the Army and over the years has expanded from leadership roles in the military, to executive roles in big business and teaching about leadership in academia.

I was privileged to be a leader in one of the great CPG (consumer packaged goods) companies in the world. PepsiCo as an international big business was not only a great place to develop as a leader, but it helped me better understand the importance of serving with and leading soldiers in combat. Following my combat tour of duty, I was nominated for and eventually selected to lead AAFES, the Army and Air Force Exchange Service, which

> *Leadership is not only about what you do, it is about who you are.*

we later rebranded as 'The Exchange'. Surprisingly, most people don't know that The Exchange is the Department of Defense's $10B for-profit retail enterprise with a unique mission to serve our nation's warriors and their families across the globe. After I left the role of CEO and Commanding General for The Exchange, I had the opportunity to be the Senior Vice President of Operations at Sam's Club leading a $15B business unit. Then I later filled a CEO role for a privately held company operating in the sales and marketing industry.

With a very few exceptions, nobody starts a professional career as top dog, CEO, President, Chairman of the Board or a senior executive of a large organization. Nor did I.

This is a book about leadership...wrapped in a personal leadership and organizational change management message. Change management at the organizational level is really a story about change leadership at the personal level. Why is this important? Because without effective personal leadership, meaningful transformational change in the organization is virtually impossible. Why is it so difficult? Because any change effort requires a change in behavior and—

The heart of effective leadership is personal trustworthiness or integrity.

as all behavior is personal behavior—that change must start with me. The most important point of differentiation among leaders is what's on the inside, not the outside. Mastering the art and science of leadership is the story of mastering self. Finding your voice leads to genuine, authentic leadership. Authentic leaders are also vulnerable leaders because they understand their own strengths and weaknesses. This is one way that self-aware leaders show their strength and confidence as influenceable leaders.

Leadership is not about title, position or place. You can lead right within your own family. Leadership is about coaching, teaching, mentoring and serving others. That is true, but it comes second. First and foremost, it is about you. We will come back to this theme again and again...it always comes back to you. It is about you, the leader, modeling the right behaviors, guided by a set of values that serve as guardrails for decision-making, setting the example, and honing your leadership style, traits, competencies and character from the Inside out. Leadership is not only or even first about challenging the organizational status quo; it is about challenging your personal status quo. One of my early lessons taught me this important point.

Story Time

I was commissioned a Second Lieutenant in 1981. I thought I was well prepared for my new leadership role in the United States Army. After four years of studying and practicing leadership in various roles and being awarded the George C. Marshall Leadership Award my senior year (the Marshall award is given to the top cadet at each university), I was confident and raring to go. My first assignment was a posting to the 69th Transportation Company in Bremerhaven, Germany.

In addition to my normal operational responsibilities, I was assigned several additional duties. Additional duties are assigned to officers and non-commissioned officers (NCOs) as a way to provide structure and oversight to a myriad of essential but routine jobs. An example of an additional duty is the "supply officer" or the "voting officer." One of the additional duties I was assigned was to lead a group of 20 soldiers to participate in the 'International Nijmegen March' held each year in Nijmegen, Netherlands. I was personally selected by our senior leaders. The selection only underscored my inflated sense of good leadership.

The march is held each year to commemorate Operation Market Garden that took place during World War II. The allied plan was to capture a number of bridges across the Dutch rivers with the hopes of breaching the German defenses in the Ruhr region. The operation was made famous by the 1977 movie, *A Bridge Too Far*. Each year members of NATO and other nations sent teams to "compete" in the marches. It wasn't so much a competition as participation with dozens of teams moving along a set route. Each soldier carried a rucksack laden with equipment and supplies. The march itself took place over four days totaling 100 miles, at 25 miles per day. Marching in formation for 25 miles a day is difficult enough, but what was really challenging was the preparation for the march. As a leader of this team (my additional duty), we marched 15-20 miles virtually every workday... over a thousand miles in all. Until then I didn't know you could get blisters on top of blisters on top of blisters. My feet were so bad that it hurt to take my boots off, and my socks were often blood soaked.

Marching everyday requires physical and mental agility. On one occasion near the end of a long day of marching, a few of the soldiers started to complain while in formation. The murmuring grew louder until one of the senior NCOs put a stop to it. Near the end of the day's march, it started all over again. I was furious. I double-timed it to the front of the formation, grabbed the private by the collar, jerked him out of the formation, and in the commotion he tripped and fell to the ground.

Not exactly how leaders model the right behaviors.

Somewhat stunned, the formation stopped and looked on. I glared down at the soldier. In those few moments I realized I wasn't anywhere near the kind of leader that I knew I could or should be, and that leadership is not about position or title. I realized I was disappointing my small team and my senior leadership. Most importantly, I was disappointing me. I knew better.

Lessons on the Basics of Leadership

Leadership is about taking others with you. Whether the team is 20 or 2,000, it is about leading from the front. In each successful organization I have worked in—the private sector, the military or academia—I have found myself coaching, teaching, and mentoring. One of my other early lessons in effective leadership is that one of the primary responsibilities of leaders is to fill the leadership pipeline by developing leaders who can make a difference in their own way.

I also recognized early on that one of the reasons coaching, teaching and mentoring is so important is because people, enabled by great systems and processes, deliver results and create value. In each organization where I effectively developed others, spent time coaching and mentoring, similar results were achieved: Better engaged teams, improved customer service, increased revenues and reduced costs, and business processes and systems improved in a measurable manner. Most gratifying, people from the top to the bottom of the organization were fully engaged and more eager than ever before to make a difference in the business. In short, they held each other accountable and owned the outcomes.

Leadership is first and foremost about you, it is personal.

I also discovered what most organizations need isn't a new program. What most organizations need are lessons on the basics that can be applied to improve engagement (culture, people and organizational health), maximize the customer experience (customer), drive better business results (performance) and create meaningful opportunities to invest in the future (innovation). Being brilliant at these basic operational tenets is a fundamental building block to sustained excellence.

The biggest and most basic of lessons—one I find people in positions of leadership often acknowledge but for which they don't really model the right behaviors or tend to forget—is that ***people*** really do matter. People are the lifeblood of organizations. They are not just assets; they are the ones creating value. Great teams are built one leader at a time, and ***effective leaders*** create a culture that enables value creation and are the #1 difference in performance and change management. Period. Full stop.

People matter; they are the life blood of every organization.

Leadership is critical because it matters at every level of every organization. Developing your personal leadership capabilities and competencies has a multiplicative or compounding effect on everything. Effective leadership improves performance, enables deeper levels of communication, commitment, and collaboration and enhances employee/team engagement which impacts organizational culture. Never underestimate the impact of leadership and the power of people performing as individual contributors or working together as part of a high performing team focused on a mission with a purpose.

They are not just assets, but they are the ones responsible for creating value.

Story Time

The Battle of Britain is considered to be the first military battle fought by air forces as opposed to purely by ground forces. The battle was fought between July and October 1940 with the German leaders focusing on destroying the Royal Air Force, so they could conduct largescale sea and airborne operations on the English mainland. With the collapse of France in June of 1940, Britain remained the lone survivor. A victory by the German Luftwaffe would open the way for Operation Sea Lion England... the invasion of England by Germany. Even though the British Fighter Command was supported by the Women's Auxiliary Air Force (WAAF) and consisted of pilots from New Zealand, Belgium France, South Africa, Canada, and the United States among others, they were outmanned and outgunned. During the battle, the British lost 792 planes and 500 pilots...nearly 1,600 Allied aircraft were lost. Axis casualties included 1,887 aircraft and 4,303 aircrews, of whom 3,336 died. You might remember this battle with one of Winston Churchill's great speeches in which he said, "Never in the field of human conflict was so much owed by so many to so few."

This story is about the triumph of the human spirit and the power of purpose. That idea can be summarized by a quote from Hermann Goering, Chief of the Luftwaffe. As the battle wore on and Axis forces continued to suffer unexpected losses and knowing that air superiority was critical for Operation Sea Lion to proceed, they were focused on the outcome and had no doubts that the superior Luftwaffe would win the day. As losses mounted and frustration grew, Hitler asked Goering what he needed to win the battle. Goering responded, "a squadron of Spitfires."

In other words, he was saying that if he had the right leaders, he could achieve victory.

Exactly!

> *Your personal leadership capabilities have a multiplicative or compounding effect on everything.*

Here is a second basic idea often misunderstood or forgotten: Leaders have followers and lead people; managers have subordinates and manage processes. There is a real, fundamental difference between the two. Certainly, both are needed in organizations, but when we don't understand and put the difference into practice, we hold people back and squash individual initiative, responsibility, and accountability.

To underscore this point, you should never, ever forget that *you lead people and manage processes.* There is no doubt in my mind that both leaders and managers are needed to drive operational excellence, but leadership comes first. I would rather have one lion with 100 engaged followers than 1,000 lambs that wander.

> *Leaders have followers and lead people; managers have subordinates and manage processes.*

Story Time

PepsiCo is a productivity factory. I learned that as a young manager there. Productivity means you can't hide from the data. As a result, you can get so focused on the 'number' that you take your eye off the ball when it comes to people and leaders. I learned it is much easier to 'manage' than it is to lead. Management tools are plentiful; data points abound; systems can act as forcing mechanisms to drive performance. Performance and data can be displayed, and management visualization tools are easy to produce and wrap your head around.

Leadership is less tangible. Leadership is developmental, not linear. It is consequential, not chronological. It is a journey with peaks and valleys. The impacts of leadership development are not immediately discernable.

During one of our annual planning cycles we were focused on delivering an annual budget that would achieve the forecasted earnings per share (EPS) number. Without a stock buy-back option, this essentially meant we would have to deliver significant productivity to make the algorithm fit. My team's share of the load was $200M over the following 18 months. We worked diligently to create strategies and supporting tactics to achieve our objectives. With the plans carefully crafted and the KPIs (Key Performance Indicators) identified, we hosted a series of planning meetings with our national team. As part of my portion of the meeting, I purchased a large stuffed monkey and made a sign that had our $200M target printed in bold colors pinned to the monkey and then strapped the monkey to my back as I gave my presentation. It was my way of adding a little humor to the meeting to demonstrate that I had a 'monkey on my back' called 'enterprise productivity'. At key points, I threw out to the audience smaller versions of the monkey with smaller dollar amounts posted to their backs (they all added up to $200M). I was making the point that we had a large target and we each had to do our share to get the monkey off our backs, so to speak. It was a big success. The team was energized to deliver on our commitment.

A few days later I got a call from one of my teammates who explained that achieving the targets we had laid out would require significant cuts in every budget item associated with people: headcount reductions, benefits, training, and leadership development. From a management standpoint, it was clear what had to be done. We needed to cut costs. From a leadership standpoint, I began reflecting on the implications to the team. Would we actually be worse off without the right people in place?

Then it dawned on me that I was thinking about the problem through a binary lens. Achieving the mandate was not an '*either/or*' proposition. Focusing on management imperatives is not achieved at the exclusion of people. Most organizations are focused on 'Doing' to achieve results, but at the end of the day sustainable excellence is determined by the quality and character of the leader. Character is what distinguishes great leaders from good managers.

In fact, I discovered both are needed to thrive in complex and ambiguous environments. Bingo! That was a great learning experience for me. This experience taught me two critical lessons:

Basic Leadership Lesson #1: People matter. They are the life blood of your organization.

Basic Leadership Lesson #2: Leaders have followers and lead people; managers have subordinates and manage process.

When you think about these lessons, you might be asking yourself, "What is leadership?" While there are many definitions, at the end of the day, leadership is about *influence*. Nothing more, nothing less. Leaders influence others to achieve an outcome tied to a purpose. Leaders influence by providing clear direction and motivation while accomplishing their mission. The Army has a great definition that captures these key components succinctly. Leadership, as defined by the United States Army is "*influencing others by providing purpose, direction and motivation while accomplishing the mission and improving the organizations.*"

Leaders have multiplicative impact on culture and performance.

So what of influence? One of the most important ways to influence others is to first be influenced. Leaders can only be influenced if they are humble and teachable. This approach implies that you understand and define for yourself what leadership is and what it is not. That you find your voice, are self-aware, and listen. For example, I noted the difference between leadership and management and that is important. But what is more important when it comes to influencing others is to understand that leadership, and subsequently my ability to influence others, starts with me. It is personal, powerful and has unlimited potential to make a difference. As I illustrated, I started to get small doses of this understanding early on in my career that shaped my thinking and subsequent development.

You lead people and manage processes.

A Few Definitions

One of the challenges in studying or discussing leadership is that of definitions. There are plenty of 'concept' words involved in understanding leadership traits and people just plain have trouble with that kind of specific definition.

Research indicates that many authors and leaders use different words to describe the same thing or use one word when they perhaps mean another. I too realize that part of learning or developing into a great leader is understanding the concepts involved. As such, here are my thoughts on character, integrity, principles and trust to clarify a few common terms and how I use and have come to live them.

Values represent core beliefs or core principles that guide your life. Values are 'what is important to you'. Values form your character in a very real sense and the direction of your decisions. They guide your behavior. God, country, family, duty and work ethic, faith, and honesty are examples of values people hold dear and use as their guides

> *Leaders influence by providing clear direction and motivation while accomplishing their mission.*

through whatever life throws at them. Your values may be unspoken but are nonetheless an important component of how people think about and describe their sense of belonging or 'Being'. In addition to personal values, organizations or groups have shared values and norms that affect how members interact and behave.

Character describes a leader's temperament, mentality, inner strength, moral or ethical code. It is the combination of your personal traits. Our character is defined by our words and actions or behaviors.

The *Oxford English Dictionary* defines character as "the sum of the moral and mental qualities which distinguish an individual or a race; mental or moral constitution; moral qualities strongly developed or strikingly displayed." Author Anthony Bell suggested that character is what enables action, stating that competencies determine what you can do, commitment describes what you want to do, but character determines what you will do.

It is your character that helps you make decisions, defines what is right and then provides a bridge to do what is right. Character combined with values gives you the courage to do what is right regardless of the circumstances or the consequences. Character, like values, is part of your 'Being' and may be unspoken but is demonstrated and visible to others through your behaviors.

Story Time

Many years ago, while I was working on my PhD, I had the opportunity to meet with Francis Hesselbein. Ms. Hesselbein has a storied history of leadership and change. She led the Girl Scouts, as CEO for over 13 years, and was the director of the Leader to Leader Institute (Formerly the Peter F. Drucker Foundation). She was awarded the Presidential Medal of Freedom and is a prolific author having co-edited over two dozen books about leadership and change.

Although I was taking copious notes that I would include in my research, there were a few things she said that have stuck with me. One of her phrases was, "the quality and character of the leader will determine performance." In addition, she came back to the premise that "leadership is a matter of being not doing." The Army and PepsiCo taught me that character is made up of two important components: character and competencies. Both are needed to deliver sustainable results.

Trustworthiness is synonymous with dependability and reliability. A trustworthy person can be counted on to behave in ways that are consistent or congruent with their own guiding principles and values. Trust provides the foundation upon which the relationship between the leader and the follower is sustained. Stephen Covey wrote that there are four legs trust stands upon: *constancy* (level headedness and staying the course); *congruity* (walking the talk); *reliability* (they have your back and do what they promise they'll do); *honesty* (true to self, word, and sense of right).

> "Speak and they will question. Do and they will follow." —UNKNOWN

Integrity and trust are often used to describe the same thing. Though integrity and honesty can be defined differently, they are often used interchangeably. From the Latin, *integrity* means soundness, completeness, wholeness. With it comes another noun, *integration*, or the act of bringing together the parts into a congruent whole and the corresponding verb, to *integrate*. Stated another way, I lead a life of integrity when my words and actions are integrated...there is no difference between what I say I will do and how I act. Broadly defined, integrity is the unswerving adherence to a specific code of behavior, that you walk your talk, that you do what you say or promise to do. Integrity is based on developing a blueprint for the future (what you ought to be) and knowing what the gap is between your best self and reality.

Principles are timeless and universal. They apply to everyone, all the time. Your principles are ways of behaving that form the framework of integrity.

Key Term	Short Description
Leadership and Management	The art of inspiring the spirit of effectiveness and the act of following. Management is concerned with the here and now, the tactics of the mission and efficiency.
Development and Succession Planning	The process whereby organizations define what types of leaders organizations need for the future and then develops systems and processes to close the gap between what the future Human Capital requirements demand.
Vision	A leader-focused, organizational process that gives the organization its sense of purpose, direction, energy, and identity.
Values	The worth one places on core beliefs. The social principles, goals or stands held or accepted by an individual, class or society. Values are grounded in principles and shape assumptions about the future.
Character	A set of qualities, mental and moral characteristics. Developing a habit of ethical traits marks a person's character.
Effective Leadership	Influencing others with honor, or stated another way, leading by living a congruent life. Effective leadership is about leading change that enhances the value of the organization, its people and programs, and it seeks to balance short-term objectives with long-term strategies.
Integrity	The rigid adherence to a specific code of behavior.

An Inside Job

How do you develop into the leader I am describing? Leadership is about influence. It is about influencing others to achieve an outcome, underpinned with a compelling purpose. It's getting others to do what you want accomplished by motivating and providing direction. But before you can influence anyone else, the first step you must take along your personal leadership journey is to 'Know Thyself'. You must develop a clear understanding of who you really are now and who you want to be at some future time. Understanding this gap is an important first step in becoming a self-aware leader.

The most effective leaders I know are individuals who are self-aware. Self-awareness means that you are able to focus on yourself (not in a prideful way) and how your values, thoughts, actions and emotions impact your own behavior and influence the behavior of others. If you are a self-aware leader, you can look in the mirror and objectively evaluate yourself, recognizing the gaps between the leader you are today versus the leader you want to become. This is the lesson I learned as a young Lieutenant and one that Max DePree (1989) underscored when he said, "The first responsibility of a leader is to define reality. The last is to say thank you. In between the two, the leader must become a servant and a debtor. That sums up the progress of an artful leader."

The first reality you must define is where you are now on your leadership journey—your current reality with all its perfections and all its lacunae. The honest application of this type of thinking implies you are humble and can be taught. Effective leaders are humble and work on their personal leadership development from the inside-out, and not from the outside-in. They recognize the biggest challenge of change is personal, not organizational.

To these genuinely effective leaders, it is first and always about developing or becoming the kind of person and leader they should become. The inside-out approach to leadership is not about developing personality traits, although they too are important, but instead it is about focusing on developing character traits. The most important personal leadership trait and personal building block is personal trustworthiness or integrity. Leadership from the inside-out is based on the idea that leaders must understand this and "get it right." It is the core, the heart, of effective leadership.

The most important personal leadership trait and personal building block is personal trustworthiness or integrity.

It is one thing to understand this idea intellectually. It is quite another to put it into practice. Earlier, I described leadership development as a personal journey. The idea of a journey applies to all leaders. You never get to the end of the journey, because as a self-aware leader, you are always discovering, growing and developing. Learning leaders are the best leaders. You're always becoming, striving, learning, and always challenging yourself to become the leader that you should and could 'BE'. You are working from the inside-out and not the outside-in. First work on developing your character traits, then your personality traits. And of those character traits, first integrity or personal trustworthiness, and then all other traits. Integrity must be carefully developed and consistently guarded because integrity problems and character flaws do not fix themselves.

> *The most effective leaders are self-aware learning leaders.*

What are some things you can do to build on this idea?

First, understand the context of the necessary change. Understand that defeating the status quo and driving sustainable change at the organizational level hinges on leaders defeating their personal status quo. It begins with 'me'. You as a leader must model the right behaviors and 'be' the kind of leader you in turn will expect others to 'be'. Without this contextual understanding, you can't lead or drive change and certainly can't sustain excellence over the long run. It simply doesn't work.

The **second** thing that enables self-awareness and hence your ability to influence, is to acknowledge you are not the smartest person in the room (even if you actually are). To openly recognize that is to also recognize the inherent value of people. It is to recognize that everybody can contribute in some way (though not perhaps your way) to a winning solution. The ancillary effect of this mindset is that it simultaneously builds trust, enhances open communication, enables engagement and stronger collaborative relationships. It demonstrates that you are influenceable, too. That simply means you are teachable, coachable, willing to learn—just as you hope others would be. As you learn to listen intently and empathically, you show that you can be influenced. They seek to complement their knowledge, skills, and abilities with other leaders. They recognize they are not the smartest people in the room, and they don't have a corner on good ideas. But you can only be influenced—can only learn and be taught—if you are self-aware and humble. As you allow yourself to be influenced, your ability to influence is strengthened. Indeed, the key to human influence is to first be influenced. The secret to getting power is to give it away.

Given that the overall goal of the leader is to improve the organization while executing the mission and delivering results. To increase effectiveness and drive change leaders must overcome the two biggest enemies of change: history and success. This requires leaders to balance, and where appropriate build on the history of success and legacy of results where it makes sense and adds value, but not be handcuffed by the past. The past should be a springboard for the future, not an anchor of the past. To move the organization forward, the leader must exercise power which is derived from giving it away. One of the hardest things for leaders to do is to relinquish control to individuals and teams. One of the hardest lessons for leaders to learn is that to get power and to be powerful, you must give it away. In a volatile, uncertain, complex and ambiguous world (VUCA) this is not a "nice to do," it is mandatory. Not only does distributed leadership build trust, confidence and credibility with the leader and followers, is the only way to win in an environment where agility and adaptability win.

At the core of both of these suggestions is the idea that the first and most important piece of leadership work is understanding, "It starts with me". I still think about yanking that young solider out of formation during that Nijmegen March. I was not leading from a mindset of integrity. I wanted to make a point and used my rank and position to make it. I was not acting from the inside-out but outside-in. It was an early leadership failure I learned from.

If I'm not a person of integrity, self-aware or influenceable or if I'm not a person who can be trusted, I must take a step backwards and refocus my developmental efforts on the thing that matters most. It is easy to point the finger of blame, but authentic leaders work from the inside-out and that means starting with me, not another. You must work on yourself before you work on others. As you do this, others notice, and your circle of influence expands. As your circle of influence expands, your ability to create excellence increases and your followership grows. Follower-centric leadership is about influence and removing obstacles so the team achieves excellence. This approach allows each team member to play to their strengths and creates a culture of collaboration, trust and learning. Leaders must be trusted. They must earn the trust and confidence of their Soldiers and followers every day. One way they do that is by serving them and articulating a compelling vision and purpose. You demonstrate that you are trustworthy by your words and actions and by ensuring they are committed to the purpose and are valued members of a high performing team. You enable execution by ensuring that they have all the resources and support needed to accomplish the mission. By doing this you help ensure that their efforts matter. Only when the team can rally around a purpose that matters can you build a culture that is purpose driven and that is healthy, has fully engaged team members and one that responds quickly, and that is agile and flexible and delivers results in the most efficient and effective way. Maintaining that culture is the work of leaders. Failure to understand this is a failure of personal leadership.

First Steps: Personal Vision and Purpose

Asking tough questions is one way to clarify your thinking. Learning to ask good questions is more important than answering them. Whether at the personal level, family level, or organizational level, the questions are basically the same:

- What do I want to be?
- What is my purpose?
- What future do I want for myself?
- What kind of person do I want to be remembered as?
- Who is the person I want to look at in the mirror every day?
- Am I the person I want to spend the rest of my life with?
- What legacy do I want to leave?

In order to gain clearer perspective on how to bring the idea of being a self-aware leader, you may need to pause and reflect. Thinking about these types of questions forces you to think deeply and clearly about the kind of leader that you want to be. Answering the questions is one way to begin focusing on what is really important to you, your purpose, and your progress. It is the beginning of your personal vision that serves as a blueprint for the future. My personal vision is something I create as opposed to a prediction. I 'predict' the future as I bring my personal vision to life by my actions.

The vision is clearly articulated so that people I lead can connect with it too, both emotionally and intellectually. The vision is my end state as a person. For the organization, it is the end result or outcome the team works toward. Your vision describes what you want to 'be'. Without a clear vision, it is impossible to create strategies to deliver the end state. It is like rearranging chairs on the deck of the Titanic…lots of activity, but of little value.

Leaders are *always* learning. Learning leaders are leaders that are maturing, growing and developing. And again, self-leadership is personal leadership and is centered around the idea that you are self-aware. The best leaders I know are self-aware. They recognize that everybody can contribute. When I am self-aware, I seek to complement my knowledge, skills and abilities with others who multiply the performance of the team. When I am self-aware, it implies that I understand my own strengths, weaknesses and leadership style. Once I know that, and communicate that to my team, I and they know how I will act. I am therefore better able to act in consistent ways, and consistency builds trust. As I build relevant relationships of trust, my circle of influence grows and my ability to influence future operations expands. That in turn helps me develop high performing teams. Being self-aware also allows me to develop a team with different styles, strengths and approaches. These complementary skill sets and styles are key enablers to driving sustained excellence. Leadership means you never rest on your laurels. You are willing and able to rise to the personal challenge of improvement: becoming more self-aware, humbler, expanding your circle of influence. In short, leadership is personal development.

Story Time

On one occasion, I was in a conversation with the leader of the multinational telecommunications company headquartered in Dallas, Texas. The purpose of the meeting was to discuss a joint business opportunity, but the conversation quickly turned to leadership.

This leader wanted to know what I thought about leadership and how he should be thinking about leadership with an emphasis on coaching and teaching his senior leaders. He described a recent business failure he thought was attributable to some larger macro industry trends (after all, it is hard to overcome the headwinds of larger industry trends). He was convinced the product launch was a failure because of the shifting market. Upon deeper discussion, he asked me for my definition of leadership. I emphasized the importance of influence and purpose. He eventually came to the conclusion the real issue was execution ... a leadership failure. We then discussed leadership in more detail and settled on a definition ('influencing others') and discussed the impact of leaders on strategy and execution.

As I've had the opportunity to travel the globe and visit with many senior leaders from the corporate and government world, I've found two common themes that crop up in most conversations. These themes apply to highly successful leaders, leaders in-the-making and even failed leaders. These two themes emerged again and again in dozens of C-suite conversations as well. The two themes are: 1) Leadership and 2) Strategies/Execution.

The first theme—Leadership—recognizes that leaders are important because they develop strategies and enable execution across the enterprise. Leaders are the drivers, the engines—the ones who relentlessly propel direction, reinforce purpose and measure performance. They are the ones who develop the next generation of leaders whose job it will be to sustain excellence. Senior leaders are deeply concerned about filling the leadership pipeline so that the strategies can be executed, and excellence sustained. Processes and systems enable, but they don't execute. People do that. Indeed, people are not "things." People create value for the enterprise, and everything else supports this value creation. And teams deliver excellence when they understand the 'what' and the 'why' and are free to develop the 'how' to achieve the objectives. Common questions that leaders ask when thinking about the importance of leadership include:

Two important themes: Do I have the right leaders? Am I executing the right strategies?

- Do I have the right leaders on the bus and are they in the right seats?
- Do I recognize their strengths and allow them to play to their strengths?
- Are my leaders in the right roles?
- Am I focused on leadership development and filling the leadership pipeline?
- Is *my own* leadership style empowering or smothering?
- Is *my own* team fully engaged?
- Does the culture support engagement, empowerment and enable excellent performance?

The second theme is about strategies which go hand-in-hand with execution. Leaders must develop strategies that can be executed. Strategies matter—big bold strategies. This is because the right strategies will build and lead to sustainable growth and excellence now and set the stage for the future. Leaders hold others accountable and develop teams that are internally accountable. Great leaders develop high-performing teams that are empowered to develop executable strategies that support the shared vision and ensure activities and supporting tactics drive the organization towards its new end state.

This implies, of course, that those strategies have milestones and underlying tactics that are measurable and can be executed. Execution is key, because in the end it's always about execution. Most leaders I know would rather have a 'B' strategy executed violently and flawlessly today than an 'A' strategy executed sometime in the future. Common questions that leaders ask about strategy and execution include:

- Do I understand the larger macro-trends in my industry? (Am I 'in touch' with current realities?)
- Am I in the right market?
- Do I have the right strategies?
- Are my strategies data-driven with insights?
- Can I execute the strategies?
- Does my approach enable agility and flexibility?

Combining these two insights about leadership and strategy/execution, I came to the conclusion that if you're not meeting your objectives personally or as an organization, it's usually one of two things.

1) Either the strategies you developed and/or their supporting metrics are not right. Therefore, be agile and flexible enough to change the strategies and act differently.
2) Or the strategies are right, but they're not being executed. That is always a leadership problem at some level.

Whether it's a leadership, strategy, or execution problem, you can trace the root cause of the issue to leaders. In fact, you must. It's easy to point your finger and cast doubt on someone else's leadership failures but remember that "leadership begins with me". Change management at the organizational level is *the story of personal change*. Without effective personal leadership, meaningful personal or transformational organizational change is virtually impossible.

Effective leadership is the combination of two things: one's character coupled with results.

I am not the first to talk about leadership in these terms. Human resource and training experts Dave Ulrich, Jack Zenger and Norm Smallwood (1999) in their book *Results-Based Leadership* state that effective leadership is the combination of two things: *one's character coupled with results*. We need both qualities to be effective leaders. We want and need leaders that set the agenda based on values. We need leaders to be values-based. More specifically, we need leaders to be grounded, rooted and centered on the idea of personal integrity or personal trustworthiness. We want leaders that deliver results and deliver those results in the right way, not leaders who deliver results by any means. The means do not justify the ends. We want leaders to deliver results in the right way, using the right metrics, based on an underlying value system. And because we are all leaders at some level, these leadership ideas are applicable to everyone.

Story Time

This point was driven home to me when I was serving as company commander of a logistics unit. I was forced to make a decision that could have ended my career. One of our routine missions was delivering sensitive and high value cargo to various distribution points. This particular mission was four truckloads of ammunition. Because of the sensitivity of this particular load, I decided to lead the effort myself. The trucks were loaded, and the convoy headed to the drop-off point.

All went well until it we arrived at the ammo dump. There was nobody there authorized to receive the load. We scurried around trying to find a responsible authority to no avail. We tried calling the emergency contact number, but again no luck. After an hour trying to find some help, I called back to the unit and talked to my boss. I explained the situation and asked for some guidance. Normally, we would bring the loads back to the unit, but because this load was ammunition and required special handling and inventory precautions, my boss told me drop the loads at the warehouse and come back. I explained again the sensitivity of the load and suggested that simply dropping it without the load being secured would be a bad decision. After further discussion he gave me a direct order: "Leave the load and come home, it's not our problem." I hung up the phone knowing I had a decision to make: Follow this order or do what I thought was right given the circumstances. I knew what had to be done. We returned to base with the ammunition. I reported to my boss with the news that I had deliberately disobeyed his order. Needless to say, he was not happy. I was threatened with a bad efficiency or performance report,

a relief of my command and a potential court martial. It was nerve-rack-
ing. But I knew I was in the right. I had acted based on principles and that
made all the difference. Over the next few days the relationship between
the two of us was tense, but he eventually realized I had made the right
call. I became one of his trusted advisors.

Where Leadership and Change Begin

You should be getting the sense that leadership is first and foremost personal.
I will come back to this theme often, and by now you too have seen these
recurring themes in the stories and concepts. You have no doubt noted that
change leadership starts first with you as a leader. Personal change is the catalyst
for organization change. As you reflect on your personal leadership consider
asking yourself these questions:

- Is the problem with my leadership? Is the crux of the problem…me?
- Am I influenceable?
- Am I developing a culture of engagement and empowerment?
- Do I model the right behaviors?
- Am I consistent in my approach? (What followers want.)

Because trust, built on personal integrity, is the glue that holds high performing teams together, we must start any change effort with a discussion on
personal leadership…the inside-out approach to leadership.

I learned this the hard way as I made that call to bring the ammunition
back against orders from my commander. I had a strong sense of what the right
thing was, and I had to do it. As a soldier, disobeying orders is no small thing. I
knew there would be consequences. I was, nonetheless, convinced I was taking
the right approach.

> *Transformational change without personal change leadership is impossible.*

Transformational change without personal
change leadership makes driving better outcomes
difficult if not impossible. Likewise, devising the
best strategies and the subsequent execution of those
strategies is impossible without effective leadership.

While there are certainly great frameworks, the challenge for leaders is
to embrace a model or a combination of models that becomes their own. It

becomes part of your DNA. You live it, repeat it, teach it a hundred times a day by your actions and language.

As leaders, we reserve the right to get smarter so that over time our ideas mature and evolve, but the basic building blocks and principles remain the same. They are 'carved in stone' as it were because they are based on timeless values and principles. It is the right combination of all of these ideas, well-learned, that enable us to look at leadership, strategy, execution in different ways and then to pick the ones that will be effective arrows in the quiver of execution. The best leaders know what arrows to pull from the quiver to align teams and achieve the best results.

I wouldn't presume that the leadership philosophy or ideas I express here in these pages are the best ones or the only ones for you to consider.

Leaders have to develop their own philosophy and must internalize that philosophy, while at the same time be able to communicate it to others. Such a philosophy is deeply personal and is a reflection of who we really are. It is about my 'being' (think vision). Once I define the kind of person or leader I want to 'be, then I can act with courage, character, and competence. More on this later, but for now, remember that values drive behaviors; behaviors drive action, and the natural fruit of action (doing something) is a result. The same thing applies to organizations. Without a clear definition of what the organization wants to 'BE', it is very difficult to drive change. A leadership philosophy is important, powerful and effective only after it becomes a personal constitution for action because as I 'DO' my 'BE' is enabled.

> *Values drive behaviors; behaviors drive action; the natural fruit of action (doing something) is a result. It all starts with values—yours.*

Having said that, I do believe there are certain fundamental building blocks of effective leadership. They apply universally because they are timeless principles. While situations and style will differ, failure to grasp the core personal traits of effective leadership will not result in either effective leadership or sustainable change at the personal or organizational level.

This brings me back to the idea that leadership is deeply personal and is a reflection of who we really are…those deep-seated values and ideas that make us who we are. It is about my 'being', or my essence and who I am. I must first define the kind of person or leader I want to 'Be' because only then can I take action and do those things that bring my vision to reality.

Story Time

I learned the importance of clearly defining the kind of leader I wanted to be when I visited Washington, D.C. early in my career. I had the opportunity to visit the nation's capital and spend some time with our political leaders. Our discussions frequently centered on national leadership and the importance of leaders to the nation's greatness. During one of those conversations in the nation's capital, the Congressman I was visiting with told a story he had read. This story made an impact on me and helped gel some of my early thoughts on what really makes a great leader.

The Congressman's story went something like this:

On a wall in the United States Capitol's basement, there is a bas-relief depicting a Greek warrior engaged in mortal combat with a snake. The artist captures the exact moment when the warrior raises his sword to strike the deathblow. Across the tableau, a single word is printed: Courage.

Artistically, physical courage is easy to depict. Moral courage is another matter. Moral courage requires taking a cold, hard look at the world and then acting, accepting the consequences, and knowing that the greatest good will ultimately be served. Moral courage demands sacrifice such as the subordination of self-interest to the interests of others. To be morally or intellectually courageous requires a basic sense of honesty and integrity coupled with the will to act decisively on those principles.

Moral character is of great importance in a leader and will inevitably affect the substance of that individual's leadership, and in the end, results.

The Congressman's story ended with this phrase, "Courage, character and performance cannot be separated." That phrase was an important 'a-ha' moment for me and helped connect the idea that leadership demands results—but also that the way the results are achieved matters. Effective leadership is the combination of all three of these elements, which are needed to deliver sustainable results in an organization.

This story helped shape my thinking and development as a leader. Leadership is not about position or place. It is about displaying certain personal characteristics and competencies that inspire and influence your followers to achieve a desired outcome. That's simple enough. Yet we struggle to achieve lasting and sustainable change. Why is this struggle so hard?

This book is an acknowledgment that personal leadership matters and that developing yourself as a leader as a continuous, life-long endeavor matters. Developing your personal leadership matters because it drives the culture, performance, and direction of any organization or team you are leading.

In the following chapters:

- I will introduce *The Leadership Circle*™—a model that describes in more detail the importance of leadership development from the inside-out as contrasted to the outside-in approach.
- I will describe in some detail the *X Factor* and the component parts of it which are vital for sustaining Xcellence: effective leadership, performance, culture (personal/organizational health).
- Finally, I will conclude with my '*Rules of the Road*'. These four rules and their twelve supporting ideas demonstrate how such a personal leadership philosophy can help you model the right behaviors and enable you to think critically about the importance of leadership as the enabling factor driving sustainable change.

2 The Leadership Circle

Another definition: Leadership: / noun /. The action of leading a group of people or an organization; different styles of leadership; the state or position of being a leader.

A 'noun'? Really? That has always baffled me.

For a word or idea with more written about it than virtually any other subject, it's puzzling to understand why the world is full of 'leaders', but so few are 'leading' (and that, decidedly, is *not* a noun).

I'll be the first to admit what the world probably doesn't need is another book about leadership and change management. If you do a search on the

Leadership is not a noun.

internet using 'leadership' or leadership synonyms and derivatives, the search results in excess of 166 million sources of leadership and millions more references about leadership ideas, definitions, and constructs. Many observers have stated the most important single underlying issue we face today is a *crisis in leadership*. And that is why there are so many leadership books: We write about it because we need it. We write about it, study it, discuss it and seek to apply good leadership because leaders are critically important in driving change and sustaining excellence…and we don't feel we have enough leaders.

Indeed, we need leaders in every type of organization. We need leaders in every organization to invest in and develop leaders. We need leaders who can articulate a future and then support that vision with supporting plans that can be executed and measured.

Leaders *influence* others to achieve an outcome by describing the purpose, direction and desired end state, and then by providing the resources and supporting culture to achieve that end state. In short, leaders give followers the *what, where* and the *why*, leaving the *how* up to the team.

Character

To become an influential leader of *character* requires a fundamental understanding of three complementary ideas.

First, you keep coming back to a fundamental idea: You evolve an ever-deeper understanding that the first and most important principle of influential leadership is that *leadership is personal.* The most important person I lead is me. At the heart of personal leadership is the notion that I can be trusted to 1) accomplish the mission and 2) take care of my team. It means I am competent, confident, and consistent. It implies personal trustworthiness or integrity… this is the heart of effective leadership. This is leadership from the inside-out.

Second, accept that personal leadership development requires a healthy dose of being self-aware. That requires honesty as you examine yourself. Great leaders recognize their strengths and weaknesses. For example, if you are self-aware, you are more likely to have an attitude of humility because you realize that you walk this good earth with countless others who are better than you are. You begin to realize you are not nearly as good as you think you are in the context of others.

- As you recognize your weaknesses and wish to further expand on your strengths, you seek to complement your knowledge, skills and abilities with that of other leaders and every one of your team members.
- As you come to this realization, you seek out others from whom you can learn. If you are self-aware, you are teachable—and this is what I call being 'influenceable'. If you can be taught, you can develop new competencies.
- As your skill set grows, you become confident in your ability to deliver results. As you consistently deliver results and grow other leaders, the consistency leads other to trust you.
- As you become a trusted agent, your ability to influence others also grows, because we are all more likely to follow someone we trust rather than someone we are cautious about. In this way, it is a virtuous circle

where development and growth in one component leads to growth in another.

Third, at the heart of effective leadership is personal integrity which I use interchangeably with personal trust or trustworthiness; leaders that act with integrity are consistent and congruent in what they say and do. When you are consistent you engender trust. You can parse the definitions, but at the end of the day, they are joined at the hip. Integrity is not just about morality or values, although they are both important and complimentary. Integrity is interactional and active, not positional and passive. Being a leader of integrity implies that I seek to integrate or to bring together individuals and teams to create value. Integrity is foundational and a fundamental focal point of leaders. It is the heart of all leadership. Period.

Character is grounded in personal integrity, trustworthiness.

To underscore the importance of character, I turn to *Nineteen Stars: A Study in Military Character and Leadership* by E. Puryear (1971), in which he selected four of America's most outstanding generals of World War II: Marshall, MacArthur, Eisenhower and Patton. Puryear used historical examples from the lives of these four acclaimed officers to make the case for all the skills leaders must develop. These skills include selflessness, willingness to accept responsibility, the ability to synthesize information and make decisions, intuition, and leading by example among others. But Puryear observed that the "greatest of all is character". Character, Puryear would state elsewhere, is "everything in leadership".

The deep-rooted notion of *character* is foundational and is built on the block of personal integrity. It impacts, colors, and influences the development of all other qualities, knowledge, skills, attributes, and traits. It is the source of one's power and defines effective leaders.

Understanding The Leadership Circle

To create a visual of what this means, I developed a model I call The Leadership Circle™ (TLC for short)[1]. This model illustrates the idea that we work from the inside-out:

---

[1] I have incorporated the findings of Marlane Miller into The Leadership Circle, adopted from *Brainstyles: Change Your Life without Changing Who You Are*, Simon & Schuster (1997).

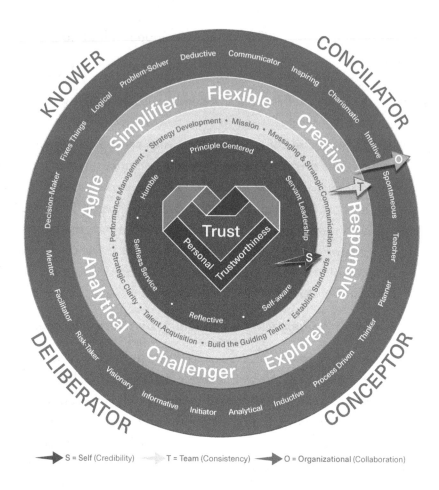

S = Self (Credibility)   T = Team (Consistency)   O = Organizational (Collaboration)

As I have studied leadership and observed leaders all around me, I have concluded that leader development is not linear; it is not a checklist that you work your way through and then declare yourself a leader. Rather it is experiential, and excellence is sequential. You are constantly and consistently working on the key elements of the circle but always working from the inside-out. The starting point, or center of the circle, is integrity or personal trustworthiness and is at the heart of the model. It is the absolute starting point that enables you to develop other character and personality traits by learning, doing, and becoming.

> Leader development is not linear and experiential, and excellence is sequential.

Moving from the inside of the TLC to the outside, I add more tools to my leadership toolbox. As the model depicts, effective leadership starts by fully understanding and developing one's character traits. It is illustrated as a series of concentric, complimentary circles where each layer builds on the previous inner circle.

In this model, you work from the inside-out, and thus start with personal trustworthiness. Once you have that characteristic firmly planted in your head and heart, then you can work to the outer edges of the TLC. You develop as a leader by working from the inside-out and building on the heart of effective leadership one concentric circle after the other.

A word of caution. The line between the numerated traits isn't entirely black and white, and there is clearly overlap. And I'm not suggesting that those traits found in TLC are the only ones you should consider developing or that one is more important than the other—with the exception of personal trustworthiness or integrity; these are non-negotiable in terms of practice or sequence! Nor am I suggesting you develop one trait before moving onto the next; that is not how we learn and grow. We develop as people and leaders in a variety of ways over a period of time.

What is important about this model is it gives you a framework to think about your leadership style and the traits that are most important to you. Also keep in mind that I do not know of a single leader who has mastered every single attribute noted in the model. I certainly am not 'there' yet.

Let's dive into The Leadership Circle. You will discover that the series of concentric circles move from character or 'Be' traits (inner circles) to personality or 'Do' traits (outer circles).

The first, red, circle moving out from the heart—where you see the traits of *'self-aware'*, *'humble'*, *'principle-centered'* and so on—is still primarily focused on you, the individual leader. These traits help you maintain and further develop the attributes of integrity and personal trustworthiness. Traits and attributes such as *humility*, *service*, *being self-aware* are other guiding principles that influence your behavior. These skills and traits are natural extensions of personal integrity. This inner red circle of qualities reflects the type of leader you want to be. They are complimentary to the heart of leadership. These traits are within you and are about your personal 'being'. As one author noted, before you ask for the hand, you have to connect to the heart. You cannot connect to the hearts and minds of people without first being personally grounded.

The Leadership Circle illustrates the idea that there is overlap between what I want to 'Be' and what I 'Do' to bring my personal vision to life. For example, the two middle rings—the gray and the light blue—illustrate the transition from Being (character traits) to Doing (personality traits and action). These represent specific actions leaders must take to drive performance and sustain excellence.

In the gray circle, you see the word '*strategy*' repeated a number of times in several contexts: **strategy, development, mission, messaging and strategic communication, strategic clarity, performance management, establishing standards**. Strategy is not something you 'are' in terms of character traits; rather, it is something you 'do'. That is associated with other skill sets and not necessarily one's character. Once I am centered and have found my voice, I am now in a position to help others find their voices. I begin to clarify the vision and mission of the organization and communicate it broadly across the enterprise. I start to develop strategies and supporting tactics that are executable, and I seek to connect execution with performance management. I begin to move from developing myself and my personal credibility to engaging and developing teams that act and deliver results consistently.

In the light blue circle, we look at other personal traits—some will already be natural to us, others we might need to learn. These traits include being a **simplifier, analytical, creative, flexible, agile, a challenger**. This stage is about developing self-control and credibility. Working from the inside-out, this blue circle compliments the personal and character traits with other knowledge and skills we can use to become even more effective. In this light blue circle, we continue to build on our skill set and are focused on building high performance teams that collaborate. We are encouraging new levels of collaboration to **create** new solutions to existing or new opportunities. The traits of this circle are proactive in nature and seek to create an **agile** and **flexible** environment where team members are focused on delivering results in the right way. We are **engaging** and **empowering** others to make a difference. We realize the power of inclusion and diversity and seek to bring the right players together to **accelerate** performance. We begin to understand that we encourage healthy debate and **analytical** decision-making, afforded to us by bringing together different perspectives and insights. This is a competitive advantage! It informs our insights and spawns **innovation** and **creativity**. We inspire the team in ways that unleashes the power of teams. In short, we play to our strengths and allow others to play to their own strengths. We leverage different styles and approaches to influence others and to achieve a positive outcome.

Information is raw material for creativity.

Finally, on the outer, darker blue edges of the circle, I recognize and continue to build on my strengths and style. I know this because I am self-aware—now I have come full-circle (no pun intended). The traits in the circle are generally aligned to support the four quadrants of the circle which are labeled on the outer edge of the image. I come to recognize that my personality falls into one of these four categories:

- The **Deliberator** is characterized by someone who assesses things first and then learns widely. A deliberator uses step-by-step analysis, is a planner, inductive. You can see where those traits are highlighted in the outer circle.
- The **Knower** can be recognized as someone who fixes things. A knower is a problem-solver, logical, deductive and usually seeks clarity first without emotion before stepping in as decision-maker.
- The **Conceptor** is a pathfinder. A conceptor is a visionary, an initiator, someone who has an idea and then tests it. The conceptor is deductive, a risk-taker.
- The **Conciliator** is a social person that inspires. A conciliator is often a caring and charismatic influencer. The conciliator can be emotional and intuitive, friendly and inductive.

As you progress on your leadership journey, you will also notice that progression implies influence. You will likewise notice that as you develop the various traits, your ability to influence others also expands. As you mature and develop as a leader, you recognize more and more that you can never take your foot of the gas pedal of personal integrity. Your ability to influence starts with you. As your credibility grows, you are then positioned to influence and lead teams. As you lead teams in a consistent manner, you set the stage to develop deeper and more relevant relationships that enable powerful organizational collaboration.

The challenge of the future is not accomplished in one great step, but rather by many measured steps along a defined path. We are on a journey, the beginning of the beginning.

The Heart of the Matter

Because leaders have a multiplicative impact on every aspect of their organizations (and more on that later), leaders must be rooted and grounded in the core of effective leadership, namely personal trustworthiness and integrity. In other words, personal trustworthiness is *The #1 Building Block* for transformational

Integrity: I lead an integrated life. My actions are aligned with my words.

change and excellence. It is the center of leadership development, and the point from which all other traits and characteristics of the leader will flow. As the model depicts, effective leadership starts from the heart of the circle. Effective leadership begins with the full understanding one's character matters.

The heart—integrity and trust—is undoubtedly the hardest to develop. It must be developed consistently and constantly. It is hard because you are always asking yourself to change. It is hard because you never 'get there' but are always working on it. You practice it every day.

When you have integrity, your words and actions are congruent and reliable—your people can count on that from you. Your people don't hold their breath to see which way your wind will be blowing, because they already know. With integrity, much of the guesswork dissolves.

Personal trustworthiness is framed by your value system, and your values are consciously thought through as you question yourself and what is important to you. Whether *family* is your top value, or *faith*, or *honesty*, or *service*—values are part of who you are and how you behave. You live and breathe them. They guide your decision-making and direct the type of goals you set for yourself. They become the solid life-building foundation. Your values in turn drive your behaviors at home, in your community, in your organization and in your daily work as you lead people and maximize performance.

Story Time

As an example of values, let me describe a place where one of my own values impacted my leadership behaviors.

Of the many experiences that have influenced my thinking and life, my deployment to the combat zone in support of Operation Iraqi Freedom (OIF) would rank at the top of the list in terms of impact.

In early 2006, I was working for PepsiCo, Inc. in a strategy and innovation role while simultaneously serving in the United States Army Reserve. In the Reserve, I was assigned as the Deputy Commanding General of a training division whose mission it was to train the Afghanistan National Army (ANA). Not everyone knows this, but about 53% of the US Army is composed of reservists or members of the National Guard—men and women like me who balance the demands of the corporate world, community and family with high visibility Army jobs.

By mid-2006 our Division had been sending units to Afghanistan for several years. Their mission was to establish enduring training institutions, as well as train and develop leaders in the ANA. While I was attending a business meeting in Chicago, my military phone rang. It was Washington with news that I was to be ordered to active duty and deployed to the combat zone. My new assignment: Commanding General (CG) of a logistics unit and the Deputy Commanding General (DCG) of the Theater Support Command (TSC). This is the type of unit that manages the supply chain.

When I got the call my first thought was, "Are you sure you've got the right guy?" The scope and visibility of the mission was expansive, and I wasn't sure I had the right competencies to be successful in ways that would earn the trust and confidence of the nation and soldiers I would serve. After the knots in my stomach finally subsided, I dove into the task at hand. I took a 12-month leave of absence (it turned out to be closer to five years!) from PepsiCo. 30 days later. I found myself standing in front of 10,000 soldiers leading the way in a faraway country.

There is nothing that humbles you more than the responsibility of command, knowing you are the guardian of America's blood and treasure, and sharing the risk of combat with young soldiers. They are magnificent in their mission, focused on the fight when called upon to do so, and they always recognize the importance of people. No wonder the Army's mantra is "Mission First. People Always."

I assumed command with full recognition I would need some help. Humility is a combat multiplier. It's a hard trait to develop and maintain because most of us think we are better than average. And paradoxically, once you start to think you are humble, the very thought implies that you are not! Humility is a hard one for leaders who think they can do it all and have little trust in the team. The help I needed came in from the thousands of soldiers doing their jobs every single day. Just as leaders have a multiplicative impact on their organization, humility has a multiplicative impact on the leader's effectiveness.

The core of truly effective leadership is based on the central idea that character—your personal character—matters when you are developing your ability to lead successfully and deliver exceptional results. It matters when you seek to influence followers who would follow you anywhere. Your character must be grounded or centered on the idea of personal integrity or trustworthiness.

Once you acknowledge this idea, enshrine it with your actions, and plant this firmly in your head and heart, your actions begin to reflect your beliefs. Then you are in a position to move to the outer edges of the circle. These skills and traits are natural extensions of personal integrity. If the heart of the Circle is about personal character traits, then the successive outer circles are more about personality traits, styles, tools, and approaches. All of these characteristics, competencies, and skills are needed to effectively execute change and leadership management.

From the Inner to the Outer Circle

By now you understand this about becoming a better and better leader: You are always focused on the *heart* of the Leadership Circle. You are always cognizant that trustworthiness and integrity form the critical foundation of great leadership. You know it is the platform from which you grow and develop along your leadership journey.

By moving from the inside circles to the outermost ones, you are consistently and continuously putting more tools in your leadership toolkit. As you do so, you learn and grow, and become even more self-aware. You begin to recognize these patterns in your own life, you begin to recognize them in others. You can set the conditions for collaboration and encourage them to play to their strengths. As a self-aware leader you too play to your strengths. And that, in turn, allows you to sustain excellence personally and organizationally. This also positions you to nurture and fill the leadership pipeline, accelerate individual and team performance, and enables a healthy organizational culture to thrive. As you spend time developing those around you, your personal influence grows, and your credibility is strengthened. You can develop others by sharing your own experiences, encouraging others to and reflect on

> *Leadership is developed from inside out, not from the outside in.*

and write about their own experiences, encourage diverse thinking, lead discussions, create their own models and leadership philosophy. As you become the leader you should be, you are in a better position to execute by developing strategies, tactics, and leadership traits needed to influence others to achieve a goal and sustain results.

tive leadership that drive and sustain performance.
Situations and styles may differ, but the basic foundational building blocks remain the same and all leaders must grasp them. Failure to understand and internalize the centering personal traits of effective leadership (located in the heart of The Leadership Circle) will result in neither effective leadership nor sustainable change at the personal or organizational level. That is why developing a leadership philosophy and recognizing that change "starts with me" is so important. Without personal leadership, transformational change and sustaining Xcellence is impossible.

Story Time

At one point I had the opportunity to lead a large retail organization. I was given a very specific mandate by the board of directors: improve the bottom line. That is a broad mandate that implies an entire series of activities. In short, improving the bottom line is the fruit of doing a bunch of other stuff right.

I spent several weeks meeting with people at all levels of the organization. I spent time listening to our customers and trading partners. I reviewed financial reports and the annual operating plan.

I then spent some time consolidating my notes and insights and developing a general framework for action. I penned a document that I titled "The Long Telegraph" (I took the name from the 1946 memo from George Kennan, the American chargé d'affaires in Moscow, describing what became the basis for America's Cold War policy of containment...it became known as the "Long Telegram", but telegraph seemed like a better fit). In my summary, I noted that change is not easy but necessary, and that we could not take for granted that our customers would continue to shop with us because of past shopping habits. The value proposition had to be clear and unassailable, and we had to deliver on the promise of the brand. I said we must turn current success into sustainable advantage.

We then hosted a series of senior leader discussions to retool our vision and supporting strategies. We engaged working teams at all levels of the organization to review the initial work and provide input. We talked to some of our customers and external stakeholders.

After several months of work, we had a 90% solution that included a new vision statement that served as a blueprint for the future. The vision statement was supported by guiding principles and underpinned by a statement of values. We identified supporting strategies, tactics, and key metrics. We realigned our HR systems to better support, performance and execution with the right Key Performance Indicators (KPIs). We developed four strategic pillars with supporting metrics:

1) Build great teams (leadership)
2) Serve our customers (customer experience)
3) Relentlessly drive execution (profitable business)
4) Invest for the future (innovation).

Thinking about the business with these priorities and in this sequence allowed the team to thrive and reframe the mandate from the board. The reframing was possible because when you build great teams (leadership) they take care of the customer, and service is improved (customer experience). As the customer experience improves, the natural consequence is that customers buy your products and services, they tell their friends about their experience and value, and the friends become new customers (profitable business). As you sell more, top-line revenue increases, margins improve and you create options that allow you to reinvest in the business, improve the value proposition, drive innovation and invest for the future (innovation).

With all that activity, the most important thing we did was ensure that we had the right leaders in place to guide the change and lead execution. This included candid conversations about performance and culture, and firm commitments about driving change. For those leaders committed to driving change, we welcomed them. For those that were not, we thanked them for their service. Driving change requires leaders to be 'all in' and to lean into the discomfort of change.

In the final analysis, leadership is about making a difference and delivering results…and sustaining a high level of performance. It is about influencing others to achieve what you want done. In short, it is delivering on your commitments (performance and culture) through people.

Further, the way results are achieved is critically important. Leaders must not only know how to get results, but how to act as well. Ulrich, Zenger, and Smallwood (1999) stated that it is not enough to master the key characteristics and attributes of leadership. Effective leaders have learned how to connect style, character, and attributes with results. Capability, they noted, must be put to use. Intent is not enough. Sustaining Xcellence requires a consistent focus on leadership, performance and culture.

The X Factor

Ulrich, Zenger, and Smallwood also proposed a formula for measuring the effectiveness of the leader, noting that effective leadership combines character and performance. Since effective leadership is the powerful combination of attributes and results, leadership is also about getting the balance right. When leaders are predisposed to focus on one part of the equation disproportionately to the other parts, overall effectiveness is diminished. Metaphorically speaking, one needs the golden eggs of results and value creation, but they cannot be achieved at the expense of the goose. You need the goose in order to get the golden eggs on the one hand, and on the other hand, any leader who loses sight of performance and is focused solely on the goose (or health and culture of the organization), won't need the goose in the long run. Therein lies the challenge.

Effective leadership has a compounding and multiplicative effect on everything the organization does. There is no way around this fact. This suggests that there are at least three implications for organizations:

- Leaders are needed at every level of the organization
- Leaders must be developed
- Without effective leadership, sustaining Xcellence is impossible and current performance suffers

You cannot underestimate the impact of leaders. It is because of this that I have specifically addressed personal leadership first. Personal leadership is the foundation of Xcellence.

What categories or types of results does the X Factor impact? Let's be clear: All of them.

- Customer experience and retention
- Top-line revenue
- Direct and indirect spend
- Outcomes
- Innovation
- R&D
- Marketing
- Stakeholder engagement
- Culture and organizational health
- Bottom-line results

All results are impacted either positively or negatively in direct relation to the leadership provided. That is why we focus so much on developing great leadership. This is why you want to become the very best leader you can be. The quality and nature of your leadership will affect the organization's results—all of them.

That brings me back to the three components of the X Factor: [2]

1. Effective leadership
2. Performance and results
3. Personal, organizational health or culture

Even though your leadership skills might be superior, all three components are needed and must be fully synchronized. They are interdependent. All three must be developed and balanced in appropriate ways to minimize risk and to sustain Xcellence. Getting this right is the essence of the leadership and change management journey. It is the right combination or balance of these three elements that drive results, improve performance and enables leaders to grow. In short, it is how individuals and organizations sustain Xcellence. But make no mistake about it: Effective personal leadership is at the heart of it all.

> Xcellence is the combination of effective leadership, performance and personal or organizational health.

[2] This idea builds on the work of Scott Keller and Colin Price in *Beyond Performance: How Great Organizations Build Ultimate Competitive Advantage* (John Wiley & Sons, 2011)

Leadership has a multiplicative impact on Xcellence.

To achieve this type of Xcellence—Xcellent results, Xcellent leadership, Xcellent outcomes—we always start at the *personal* level and develop a deep understanding of how our own *personal leadership* impacts both the health and the performance of the organization.

The Metrics of Sustainable Xcellence

To illustrate the mechanics of the X Factor, let me describe how its math or metrics work.

The formula uses the numerical responses to a series of questions. There are 18 questions, broken into three sections that correspond to the three elements that sustain Xcellence: Leadership; Performance; Health/Culture. Each of the three key components is part of the calculation: L for Leadership, P for Performance and H for Health/Culture. Use a 10-point Likert scale for each component, with 1 being the lowest rating and 10 the highest. Your score is calculated and then plotted on the sustainability matrix. The questions can be found at the end of this chapter.

You can take a quick look now to get a general feel for the questions. You don't need to perform an in-depth survey or study to answer these questions—you inherently know the answers to them. After you have answered all 18 questions and calculated the average in each of the three areas, you can then use the following formula to make the calculation.

Described mathematically, the X Factor or Xcellence is expressed in this formula:

$$f(x) = (L) \times (P{+}H)$$

Sustained Excellence (X) is a function (f)' of:

– Leadership (L (both positive and negative))
– multiplied by (x)
– the performance (P) of the organization
– plus (+)
– the culture or health of the organization (H or O)

Let's do all that math with an example. Again, once you have answered all of the questions you simply rate yourself on each of the 18 questions in each of the three categories, score each category, then take the average of the three scores for your total.

As an example from your responses to the 18 questions:

- You determine that you have great **leadership (L),** with an average score of **8.** Since we are using the ten-point scale, an **8** is indeed terrific!
- You continue with your **performance (P)** average score, which is a **4.**
- You assess your personal or organizational **health (H)** at an average score of **3.**
- Using the formula, that total comes from this calculation: **(8 x (4+3))**
- Doing the math your total "X Factor" score would be **56.**

Consider the same example with poor leadership (L)—say you have an average score of **2.** Doing the math again using the same scores on (P) and (H), my new total score would be **14 (2 x (4+3)).** This is clearly a *significantly* lower score because effective leadership is a personal or organizational *multiplier.* The lower the leadership (L) multiplier number, the lower the total score. Of course, a "zero" in leadership implies a "zero" in the formula: no leadership, or toxic leadership, means that Xcellence is simply not sustainable.

Pulling It All Together

What does the result of this formula really mean to you as a leader?

- The *lower* the total X Factor score, the lower the probability that either personal or organizational Xcellence can be sustained. Short-term results are certainly achievable but sustaining them is the key.
- Conversely, the *higher* the scores, the better your chances that Xcellence can be sustained.

At the personal level, the same rule applies. It is one thing to go to a seminar or a week-long training event and get psyched up. It is another thing to fundamentally change the way you think and act and sustain those changes over time.

There is no doubt that effective Leadership has a multiplicative impact on Xcellence. Leadership impacts every facet of our lives and organizations. If you want great performance and engaged teams—develop leadership. Based on your total score and the specific elements of your score, you can determine the areas that need developmental focus.

As others take the survey, you can review those scores and use that data to take a deeper look by functional team, tenure or level, and to analyze what transformational elements are required to improve. Understanding the makeup of the three components helps shape needed strategies and points you towards a starting point and priorities.

Continuing the Metrics

Overall

Leadership

Performance and Org. Health	0	1	2	3	4	5	6	7	8	9	10
0	0	0	0	0	0	0	0	0	0	0	0
1	0	1	2	3	4	5	6	7	8	9	10
2	0	2	4	6	8	10	12	14	16	18	20
3	0	3	6	9	12	15	18	21	24	27	30
4	0	4	8	12	16	20	24	28	32	36	40
5	0	5	10	15	20	25	30	35	40	45	50
6	0	6	12	18	24	30	36	42	48	54	60
7	0	7	14	21	28	35	42	49	56	63	70
8	0	8	16	24	32	40	48	56	64	72	80
9	0	9	18	27	36	45	54	63	72	81	90
10	0	10	20	30	40	50	60	70	80	90	100
11	0	11	22	33	44	55	66	77	88	99	110
12	0	12	24	36	48	60	72	84	96	108	120
13	0	13	26	39	52	65	78	91	104	117	130
14	0	14	28	42	56	70	84	98	112	126	140
15	0	15	30	45	60	75	90	105	120	135	150
16	0	16	32	48	64	80	96	112	128	144	160
17	0	17	34	51	68	85	102	119	136	153	170
18	0	18	36	54	72	90	108	126	144	162	180
19	0	19	38	57	76	95	114	133	152	171	190
20	0	20	40	60	80	100	120	140	160	180	200

< 30%   30%   50%   60%

Once you know your X Factor score, look at the percentages on the sustainability matrix above. In our example, a total score of **56** would indicate that there is about a **30%** chance of success in terms of sustaining Xcellence. Turn that upside-down, and you have a **70%** chance of not sustaining it…not good odds.

You'll notice some overlap in the scores—you see that there is more than one '56'. The reason for this is that all three components impact the outcome and chances of success in different ways, but generally they fall within a color-coded area or range that is directionally correct. For example, you might have stronger leadership and worse performance or organizational health numbers but still be within the 30% range. Again, I want to emphasize that the data points are directional in nature. Even if you scored a perfect 200, a high score does not guarantee excellence can be sustained. It is designed to give you a sense of the probability of success.

Finally, a word of caution. The matrix and questions are based on a variety of sources and traditional literature reviews, research, my own observations and relevant practical experience over many years. As such, and from an academic standpoint, this model is limited because it is not built on established practices of rigorous research that test for validity and reliability. The important thing is this: Like the Leadership Circle, it is a framework to get you thinking.

**There are three vital components for sustaining excellence.
A leader is responsible for them all.**

Once you have a good understanding of your X Factor score, you can glean the following insights:

1. Leaders have a compounding effect on everything, including performance, but excellent leadership alone, with no supporting business processes to drive performance and a culture of collaboration, is not enough.
2. The sustainability matrix suggests that with scores above 100 there is a 60% chance that change will stick and Xcellence be sustained. But note this: While 60% is a relatively low number in terms of achieving performance targets, in the realm of change management and change leadership, it's a *very high* score and an indicator of success.
3. The X Factor score you arrived at with the 18 Question survey is only directional in nature. There is always work to be done.
4. While short bursts of excellent performance can be generated, sustaining that performance requires the right combination of all three components: Leadership, performance and a culture that is engaging and empowering. This is the job of the leader!

Consistency and Clarity

Most leaders, though well intended, aren't consistent in their leadership approach, their philosophy of leadership, or how they describe leadership. Frankly, they just are not clear in their own head about it. Your leadership philosophy is your narrative about what you believe and how you will lead. It is a framework that allows you to be consistent in your approach and helps ensure you deliver what every follow needs: consistency, hope, trust and stability (See *Strengths Based Leadership* by Tom Rath and Barry Conchie for a deeper understanding of follower needs).

I discovered that most people don't have a good way to summarize what they believe and why they believe that way. That is why I spent a good deal of ink on this in the first two chapters. When you ask a leader to describe his or her leadership philosophy you usually get a laundry list of specific attributes or ideas like this one:

1. It ain't as bad as you think; it will look better in the morning.
2. Get mad, then get over it.
3. Avoid having your ego so close to your position that when your position fails, your ego goes with it.
4. It can be done!
5. Be careful what you choose; you may get it.
6. Don't let adverse facts stand in the way of a good decision.

You may recognize this partial list as belonging to former Secretary of State Colin Powell, whom I greatly respect and admire. I consider him one of the great leaders of character in this century. However, that is not the kind of 'list' I believe a leader should have to describe his leadership philosophy.

Lists are well and good as far as they go. I actually like many of them. If you boil them down to their essence, they share many common themes. Yet as good as they might be as guides to leaders-in-the-making, there is no silver bullet, magic wand, buzzword, flow chart, book or single idea that you can read and say, "*That's* what leadership is all about." No list is powerful enough to change behavior.

Leadership is first *personal.* It starts within you. The lists you read about, whoever they are from, are *personal.* They have been developed over a period of time and tested in the crucible of stress and action. What makes them great and unique is that their originators have thought about their list, really thought about it; they own them; when they talk about them, you can sense their passion and commitment.

But the one thing missing from most lists and statements of philosophy is the reason behind it. What is the reason for the list, the whys-and-wherefores of it? What is the connection to a larger purpose, reason, or personal voice?

Leadership is not developed by using a list or reading a book. These are good starts but not the end of the journey. That is not how leadership development works. We call it leadership 'development' for a reason. Leaders are developed, grown, taught, trained, educated, challenged, tested—and they evolve—by a variety of means. These could include developing an understanding of how you sustain Xcellence using an assessment tool like the 18-Question X Factor survey, or other assessment tools like 360 feedback, a personality assessment, good coaching and mentoring and perhaps most importantly key assignments. Understanding where you are today and comparing that to where you want to be will stretch your thinking and capacity. As self-aware leaders we are all on a journey…learning, doing, and becoming better. We are always evolving as leaders.

18 Questions

A Personal and Organizational Questionnaire

Personal

Leadership

Question	Score	Comments/Notes
1. Do you have a clear vision of what you really want to "BE" (Your Best Self)	1—2—3—4—5—6—7—8—9—10	Can you clearly define your purpose?
2. Do you have a plan to achieve your "BE"?	1—2—3—4—5—6—7—8—9—10	Do you know your BFT?
3. Do you have a clear understanding of your strengths and weaknesses?	1—2—3—4—5—6—7—8—9—10	
4. Do you "play to your strengths" everyday?	1—2—3—4—5—6—7—8—9—10	
5. Do people seek you out for advice and guidance?	1—2—3—4—5—6—7—8—9—10	
6. Can you articulate your leadership philosophy?	1—2—3—4—5—6—7—8—9—10	
Average Score		

Performance

Question	Score	Comments/Notes
1. Do you set goals that stretch your personal capacity and capabilities?	1—2—3—4—5—6—7—8—9—10	Are my goals tied to my priorities and purpose?
2. Are your goals tied to your personal vision (your "BE" / best self)?	1—2—3—4—5—6—7—8—9—10	
3. Do you have a way to track how you are progressing?	1—2—3—4—5—6—7—8—9—10	Can you break your goals into bite-size segments?
4. Do you hold yourself accountable for achieving your goals?	1—2—3—4—5—6—7—8—9—10	
5. How often do you achieve your personal goals?	1—2—3—4—5—6—7—8—9—10	
6. Do you review your progress frequently?	1—2—3—4—5—6—7—8—9—10	
Average Score		

Personal Health

Question	Score	Comments/Notes
1. How often do you recognize others for their contributions?	1—2—3—4—5—6—7—8—9—10	Do I recognize the value of people in my life?
2. How important is failure and are you resilient?	1—2—3—4—5—6—7—8—9—10	
3. Do you feel you have the right balance in your life?	1—2—3—4—5—6—7—8—9—10	
4. Do you recognize that your values drive your behaviors?	1—2—3—4—5—6—7—8—9—10	
5. Do you have an overall sense of optimism about the direction of your life?	1—2—3—4—5—6—7—8—9—10	
6. Do you set goals in the following six areas: Physical, Mental, Family, Spiritual, Personal, Financial	1—2—3—4—5—6—7—8—9—10	
Average Score		

Organizational

Leadership

Question	Score	Comments/Notes
1. Is the quality of engagement with customers, suppliers, partners and others (external) designed to drive value?	1—2—3—4—5—6—7—8—9—10	
2. Is the vision and mission of the organization well understood by all team members?	1—2—3—4—5—6—7—8—9—10	Is the organization purpose driven?
3. Does the organization have a well-defined leadership philosophy or model?	1—2—3—4—5—6—7—8—9—10	
4. Are all team members playing to their strengths and have all the resources they need to get the job done?	1—2—3—4—5—6—7—8—9—10	
5. Is the talent acquisition process designed to attract, hire and develop the best leaders?	1—2—3—4—5—6—7—8—9—10	
Average Score		

Performance

Question	Score	Comments/Notes
1. Are individual and team performance objectives developed to support the organizational strategies?	1—2—3—4—5—6—7—8—9—10	Are the strategies aligned with the vision and purpose?
2. Does the organization have clear understanding of its capabilities and leveraging them to drive a result?	1—2—3—4—5—6—7—8—9—10	Are resources allocated correctly?
3. Do individuals in the organization understand what is expected of them and how they will be measured?	1—2—3—4—5—6—7—8—9—10	Are the team members fully engaged?
4. Are team members held accountable for results?	1—2—3—4—5—6—7—8—9—10	Are the team members empowered (accountable and responsible)?
5. Are the key performance objectives frequently reviewed and discussed?	1—2—3—4—5—6—7—8—9—10	
6. Are our strategies and supporting tactics aligned across functions and designed to achieve the vision?	1—2—3—4—5—6—7—8—9—10	
Average Score		

Culture/Organizational Health

Question	Score	Comments/Notes
1. Is there a process or forum to recognize team members on a frequent basis?	1—2—3—4—5—6—7—8—9—10	
2. Do team members understand how "innovation happens" and ideas get implemented?	1—2—3—4—5—6—7—8—9—10	
3. Would you recommend this organization as an "employer of choice" to your friends? Is the team fully engaged (two part question)?	1—2—3—4—5—6—7—8—9—10	
4. Do team members and senior leadership generally embrace change or resist it?	1—2—3—4—5—6—7—8—9—10	
5. Is there a shared set of values that drive behavior?	1—2—3—4—5—6—7—8—9—10	
6. Is there an overall sense of optimism about the organization that drives team members to put forth their best effort in achieving results?	1—2—3—4—5—6—7—8—9—10	
Average Score		

PART TWO

The Four Rules of the Road

In Part One, I discussed the heart of leadership, and how and why it is personal. Effective leadership is first and foremost about the character of the leader—the leader's 'BE', so to speak. The heart of character is based on personal values, personal trustworthiness or personal integrity, with trust being the glue that holds high performing teams together. Said another way, becoming a trustworthy leader is also about becoming a person of Xcellence. It is about me 'becoming' the kind of person and leader I know I can and should be.

In Part One, I demonstrated how leaders have a personal, direct, defining, lasting, and multiplicative impact on the results and the culture of the organization. Your personal leadership will impact the group's Xcellence—in the moment and in the short, middle and long term. What leaders *do* usually gets more 'ink' because activity is easy to measure and track. That is also the reason why I felt it vital to begin with the much ignored 'BE' of leadership and the impact leadership has in our personal lives, communities, churches, and nation.

In Part Two, I will get into how you translate your 'BE' or your vision into 'DO' or your actions. It is one thing to 'be' a person of integrity and another to 'do' something that creates value. Leaders make a difference by how they execute or carry out strategies and plans of action that lead them, their organizations and teams to the desired end state. The two aspects—BE and DO—are interdependent and entwined to create those sustainable Xcellent outcomes.

To demonstrate that BE/DO synergy, in the next chapters I present *4 Rules of the Road*. The 4 Rules model will deepen your understanding of the personal BE aspects of leadership while demonstrating how the DO aspect operates in tandem with it to achieve and sustain Xcellence. By working from the 4 Rules, you deepen your personal leadership capabilities which then improve your ability to personally influence the people, results and culture of the organization.

4 Rules of the Road: A Leader's GPS

To begin to overcome and take advantage of the challenges of personal and organizational change, I developed a leadership philosophy that I call my 4 Rules of The Road. The model is graphically depicted here:

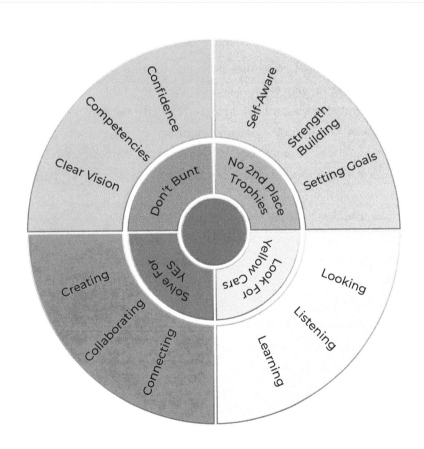

To generate sustainable Xcellence, leaders must be clear on their intent, articulate a compelling vision and purpose, identify key supporting strategies and then align resources to execute. Leaders learn, DO and BEcome better when they practice these skills and develop the supporting competencies.

Story Time

My spouse and I have five children and, as all parents know, things could get hectic at home. Between early morning band, after-school sports, homework, play time, piano and dance lessons, you try to throw in a little personal time and the day is gone.

Like all parents, you want your kids to learn and grow into responsible adults. But there are days when you are absolutely positive either you or they will not survive the night, let alone turn into a responsible generation. You try and teach your children the importance of decision-making and the consequences of decision-making. In our family, we would often say, "every choice has a consequence and every consequence has a destination".

We love our children to make choices, especially if the choice they make is the same choice we would make. When that happens, we pat ourselves on the back and say, "good parent". However, when a choice is made that isn't exactly what we would do, we are quick to point out the consequences. Even though we want our children to learn by their mistakes, it is a painful process. Life would be so much easier 'if only our children would listen!'

To help guide children, many families have 'family rules.' You know some of them: Be home by 11 p.m.; no phones after 10 p.m.; homework before play; clean your room. These are generally good ideas as long as our children understand the 'why' of the rules and they really are left to make a choice.

A clean room is at the top of my list. How many times have you asked (told) your children to clean up their rooms? After a little back and forth, the child reluctantly cleans the room, you inspect, thumbs up, looks great...only to return a few hours later or the next day to find the room in the same disastrous condition. The same conversation takes place and the cycle repeats itself.

Wouldn't it be more powerful and lasting if the child understood an underlying principle about personal discipline? Obviously your 2-year old doesn't really care about personal disincline but hear me out. If you can teach a child about the importance of leading an organized and disciplined life, the natural fruit of that core understanding is a clean room. If that idea is understood and lived, you never have to ask your children to clean their rooms again. A clean room is simply a natural consequence of personal discipline.

Of course, teaching these principles takes time. Some of it will stick and some won't, but the point is: Teach the right principles, be a model of the right behavior, and magic happens.

In the Thurgood family, we dutifully started out with a set of family rules, and as the family grew and aged, we would change them—until one day I had an insight that reshaped my thinking...and we got rid of all the rules!

Since that day, we have two simple rules. Only two. I call them the **Two Rules of Life**. Understand and live these two rules and you can't go wrong. They are empowering and enabling. Ignore them and peril is in your path.

- The first rule is: DO what you are supposed to do.
- The second is: BE where you're supposed to be (not just a physical location... BE the kind of person you know you should be).

When our kids would ask for permission (their way of saying, "I know what I should do, but I need mom or dad to tell me I can or cannot do it so that my actions are justified"), we would just ask two simple questions: Is that what you should be *doing*? Is that where you are supposed to *be*?

We didn't always get the answer we wanted, but we saw that it started to help the children develop a sense of ownership for their lives and that it was empowering them.

The BE part of the rule is more than just a physical location you are in. Our kids grasped that it is about *be*ing and *be*coming the kind of leader, person, sibling, classmate, student...that you need to be, should be, can be. They were being guided to build their own personal Xcellence.

They got that **be**ing is brought into reality by **do**ing. They began to turn more and more right actions into results that moved them towards their personal vision. They understood that sustaining that action over a long period of time was the second piece of personal Xcellence. Doing and being became mutually supportive.

Leaders DO and BEcome better when they practice these skills and develop the supporting competencies.

Once we understand the value of defining our BE and the impact that DOing the right things has on BEing the best person we can be, we begin to capture the essence of change. You must be the change you want to see. You model the way. Those two ideas that had their genesis in the heart of my own family eventually led me to think about leadership in a new light. Over time, I developed my 4 Rules of the Road that are all about DOING and BECOMING.

Just as at the personal level—in my family and in me—change starts with the questions of being and doing. Change at the organizational level starts with the questions of Where, What, Why:

– Where are we going?
– What does the future look like there?
– Why are we going there?

This is an important point because leaders drive change, and the first change that must take place starts with the leader—with me, at the personal level. Once I am clear on my BE, I can move into the DO circle and take relevant actions; I can DO things that support my BE. You always work from the inside-out, not from the outside-in as most people think.

– At the personal level, leaders answer the question, "What do I want to BE? What is my personal vision? What are my strengths and gaps? Am I accountable?"
– At the organization level, the questions leaders answer are, "Where are we going and why are we going there? What is our vision? Is the team fully engaged? Do we hold each other accountable?"

The Why, What, Where and Be are hard questions to answer! You must get these right and it is often a matter of 'going slow to go fast'. You don't want to rehash or rework the vision statement frequently, so take time and care upfront to formulate it. Once those questions are answered in detail and with clarity of thought, the next step is to recognize what I must DO to become the person I described in my BE.

The same concept applies to organizations and that is what I have done through my 4 Rules of the Road.

Much like we guided our children to live with our two simple rules of BE and DO, leaders guide their teams to Xcellence according to a structure. The 4 Rules of the Road model describes such a process. It starts with the premise of *personal leadership* and *sustained Xcellence* and provides a framework to *turn that into action*.

In the 4 Rules of the Road, all of the elements required to achieve transformational change at any level (personal, team, organizational), are embedded in one of these three ideas:

1. Leadership
2. Performance
3. Culture / Organizational health

It Didn't Happen in a Day

I've developed these 4 Rules of the Road and the accompanying concepts over a period of years. On my way to finalizing them, I've had my list of 13 'things' that make a leader…the 'baker's dozen of must do's' for great leaders. Over time, I added to and subtracted from the list, but what I found in the end, it was still just a list…things I learned by observation and the school of hard knocks.

While the 'list' would make perfect sense to me, I also recognized was that it wasn't easy to explain the ideas to people on my team in easy-to-understand language they could connect with emotionally and intellectually. I wanted them to remember and apply the ideas. I wanted them to internalize the concepts and more importantly begin to develop their own Rules of the Road that would drive action and behavior changes.

You have more detail around each of the 4 Rules in coming chapters, but for now here they are:

1. Don't Bunt
2. No Second Place Trophies
3. Look for Yellow Cars
4. Solve for Yes

The 4 Rules of the Road are the four big building blocks of the model, and though they are meant to build on each other, they are just as powerful as standalone ideas.

For example:

- **Rule #1** — when I get up to the baseball plate and swing hard, I show that I can and am willing to step out boldly and take risks. (Rule #1, "Don't Bunt").
- **Rule #2** — as I step out and swing hard, I show I have a determination to sustain Xcellent performance, backed by my word and deed. (Rule #2, "No Second Place Trophies").
- **Rule #3** — as I come to recognize that I'm not the smartest guy in the room (self-awareness), I learn from others. (Rule #3, "Look for Yellow Cars").
- **Rule #4** — as I listen and learn, I am open to new ideas and new solutions and new ways of thinking. I value diversity and inclusion. That, in turn, leads to creative ideas that are better than any single solution that either you or I may come up with as individuals (Rule #4, "Solve for Yes"). As I create and implement those innovation solutions with my team, I build trust and credibility with myself and them.
- High trust enables me to therefore 'swing hard', (a return to Rule #1) because I have developed the character and competencies needed to make and keep commitments (a return to Rule #2). I am a trusted agent; I can underwrite mistakes. Competence builds confidence. When I am confident, I can boldly deliver on what I say I'm going to do (a return to Rules #1 and #2).

I think of these 4 Rules as simple building blocks of Xcellence that move me and my team forward.

As a leader, I must understand things as they really are, and of course realize that leadership is personal first and foremost. If I am self-aware and have a good understanding of my strengths and weaknesses, I focus first on myself or work on my self-mastery. I must always recognize that both the opportunity and the problem are mine, not somewhere out there.

By the way, using the word self-mastery is a little bit of a misnomer because you never really 'master' yourself. Self-mastery is a journey, not a destination. You are always learning, growing, developing, and changing in positive ways. The idea is always that I will work first on myself. I understand my strengths and my weaknesses. I understand the reality, and I see the gap between my actual performance or actions and where my stated personal vision is. When I begin to see the 'true' me, I recognize I'm not as good as I think I am. When I truly recognize that, I become a humble servant-leader.

There is a great poem titled "The Indispensable Man" by Saxon Kessinger that captures this thought:

Sometime when you're feeling important;
Sometime when your ego's in bloom
Sometime when you take it for granted
You're the best qualified in the room,

Sometime when you feel that your going
Would leave an unfillable hole,
Just follow these simple instructions
And see how they humble your soul;

Take a bucket and fill it with water,
Put your hand in it up to the wrist,
Pull it out and the hole that's remaining
Is a measure of how you will be missed.

You can splash all you wish when you enter,
You may stir up the water galore,
But stop and you'll find that in no time
It looks quite the same as before.

The moral of this quaint example
Is do just the best that you can,
Be proud of yourself but remember,
There's no indispensable man.

My 4 Rules of the Road are designed to remind me that improvement is a journey—and the Rules are my GPS all along the way. Humility is one of the leader's best qualities, and there is always work to do on becoming your best you.

Here I summarize my *4 Rules of the Road*. Note that each one is accompanied by three **KSAs**—an acronym that stands for ***Knowledge, Skills, and Abilities***.

1. **Don't Bunt**: When I get up to the plate, I need to swing hard unless the coach tells me to bunt. On occasion there may be a good reason to bunt because the team wins, but otherwise when I get up to the plate, I will be swinging hard, doing my best to step out and be bold. When I do my best, I leave a legacy of Xcellence and belong to the fellowship of the doers.

   The three **KSAs** are: **C**larify vision, define **C**ompetencies, build **C**onfidence.

2. **No Second Place Trophies**: In my life, in everything I do, I strive for Xcellence. That doesn't mean I always get it right, but it does mean that I seek Xcellence in all I do: in my life, my family, my community, and my business. It means that I lead out; I am a pioneer, not a settler.

   The three **KSAs** are: be **S**elf-aware, build on my **S**trengths, **S**et goals.

3. **Look for Yellow Cars**: This is a simple metaphor for saying "Pay attention". In other words, I realize I am not as smart as I think I am, and I'm not as good as I think I am. Nobody has a corner on good ideas, and none of us is as smart as all of us. This is an idea that encourages me to look for things that I would not ordinarily look for. When I do that, I learn to listen, to look, and to learn.

   The three **KSAs** are: Look, Listen, Learn.

4. **Solve for Yes**: The world is full of naysayers and those who say "no" to me simply because they can. Maybe they don't solve for yes because it will cause more work or disrupt their perceived status quo. Or maybe there just isn't enough emotional energy, edge, or intellectual curiosity to move things along. There are times when a "no" is appropriate, but by and large, I will strive to be part of the solution and not part of the problem.

   The three **KSAs** are: **C**onnecting, **C**ollaborating, **C**reating.

The challenge before us is this: How do you create a game-changing paradigm that leapfrogs the current glide path you are on, and puts you on a completely different path to the future? And not to just any future but to a *better, consciously designed* future?

> *Nobody is as good as they think they are, and nobody is as smart as they think they are.*

- We need a framework that creates a new BE
- But we also need a way to DO things differently
- We need a framework that all can connect with intellectually and emotionally
- We need to create a paradigm that is simple yet powerful, and that anybody can understand, teach—and follow
- We need individual leadership that allows everyone to play to their strengths
- Finally, we need a framework that perpetuates itself and becomes part of our generational legacy

My *4 Rules of the Road* work for me and give a framework to leave a legacy. Let's get into them!

5 Rule of the Road #1: Don't Bunt

One of the reasons you bunt in baseball is to advance the runner. There are variations of the bunt: the squeeze play, the sacrifice bunt, the drag bunt, the suicide squeeze. Many consider bunting 'old school' and prefer to focus on the 'long ball'. In fact, on average there is about one bunt for every four games. Batters only bunt when the coach gives the signal to bunt, otherwise players swing away, hard, at the plate.

Although it's a great metaphor, this first rule of the road—"Don't Bunt"—is not about baseball. It is about taking bold action to change the outcome. Swinging hard means being a pioneer, leading out, going for it, being bold, stepping briskly and confidently into the future.

Most people don't show up to work to fail. They want to do a great job but often lack the resources or support to accomplish the mission. People want to do well, finish the goal, and make a difference.

"Don't Bunt" is about DOing. Leaders don't bunt! They swing and swing hard! They create cultures so that others can swing hard, too. Most people will swing hard and act boldly when they know failure is 'only' a developmental tool and not a reason for punishment or ridicule. When they know that failure is a tutor and not a tragedy. When they embrace the truth that failure is a teacher and not a teaser.

When you ask others to swing hard, you must be able to underwrite, exploit, and mitigate risks. "Don't Bunt" leaders are accountable, responsible and empower others to deploy the same accountability and responsibility. These types of leaders think big, set and enforce high standards. They have a bias for action.

Bold leaders are transformational leaders. Bold leaders build trust. Bold leaders are engaging, enthusiastic, and enabling. Bold leaders defeat the status quo and create a culture of Xcellence.

You enable others to swing hard by practicing these three **KSAs** (knowledge, skills and abilities) and developing them as habits of Xcellence:

1. **C**larify vision
2. Define **C**ompetencies
3. Build **C**onfidence

The three KSAs all have a C in them to associate them with this Rule of the Road. Also note the sequence: As I *clarify* the vision, I can then build *competencies* to develop strategies and tactics to deliver that vision. As I consistently deliver results, I build personal and organizational *confidence.*

Nobody succeeds alone.

Let's look at each KSA in turn, and how each one bolsters this Rule of the Road about taking bold action.

Clarifying and Sharing Vision

Developing strategic clarity is asking, "Where Do You Want to Go?"

One classic story illustrates the importance of being grounded in reality and providing important insights about purpose and direction. Lewis Carroll wrote a children's novel titled *Alice's Adventures in Wonderland* (written nearly 160 years ago in 1865 at the end of the Civil War—and still relevant today). In the book, Alice learned an important lesson as she was searching for a way out of Wonderland and came to a fork in the road. "Would you tell me, please, which way I ought to go from here?" she asked the Cheshire Cat. "That depends a good deal on where you want to get to," the cat responded. Alice replied that she really did not much care. The smiling cat told her in no uncertain terms, "Then it doesn't matter which way you go."

Your leadership moment will be defined by the direction you choose. Remember what Andy Stanley said, "Everyone ends up somewhere in life. A few people end up somewhere on purpose. Those are the ones with vision."

Michelangelo was right. He was once asked what made him a great sculptor. Paraphrasing what he is purported to have said, "The perfect form lies concealed in the block of stone, all that's needed is to chip away until it is revealed."

So it is with each of us. We are all people of potential. Hidden beneath our sometimes rough and ugly exterior lies a leader; underneath a seemingly one-dimensional surface lies someone who is

Failure is a tutor, not a tragedy.

multifaceted, multitalented and who can make a difference; underneath lies someone with unlimited potential who has a true spark of deity.

Knowing where you're going is important. Without that clarity, how can you have confidence that the strategies you are executing and the resources you are allocating are driving you towards your end state vision? Short answer: You can't. If you are unclear about what you want to BE, either personally or organizationally, without a clear vision, developing strategies and aligning resources and effort is an exercise in futility. You may feel good about the activity, the daily grind, but in the end the activity is just that…activity, doing for the sake of doing.

A compelling vision builds trust, inspires confidence, enables collaboration, is interdependent, is motivational, and requires mutual accountability for success. A vision helps teams and individuals make smart choices, because their decisions are being made with the end result in mind. As goals are accomplished, the answer to "What is next?" becomes clear. Vision allows people to act from a proactive stance, moving toward what they want—rather than reactively away from what they don't want.

Knowing where you're going requires a clear, purpose driven vision. A clear vision is so persuasive and so compelling that you must move toward it. A clear vision builds trust, inspires confidence, enables collaboration, is motivational, and requires mutual accountability for success. Vision and leadership are interdependent. When you work from a sense of purpose and align your priorities to achieve that purpose, you are well on my way to achieving excellence.

Interdependence of Vision and Leadership

Like a well-composed symphonic score, vision and leadership unfold in synergy to motivate, inspire, and move people and organizations forward. A leader must have a vision, but also a supporting plan to turn that vision into action and reality.

To defeat the status quo and drive positive change, leaders must define the current reality. From that scenario, they then craft a compelling vision, articulate the 'why' of the change—all the while creating a sense of urgency enabled by strategies which are agile, flexible, and well-resourced.

From a business point of view, such a vision describes a value proposition and purpose so compelling that customers and trading partners immediately see the value added by business proposals and align their external teams to support the initiative.

Vision, Strategies, Resource Allocation

The vision drives the organization's transformational change. As such, you cannot disconnect effective personal and organizational leadership from change efforts or sustained Xcellence. Once the current reality is clearly defined and you have taken a good hard look at yourselves or at your organizations…once you recognize the truth, you begin to get a sense for the performance gap between where you or the organization is now, and where you are going.

Go slow to go fast. Take time to clearly define your vision and purpose.

A vision is a blueprint for the future. It is directional in nature and aspirational. It is bold. Creating a vision starts with describing a future that is different from the current trajectory. Once you have the end state clearly defined, you must then be brutally honest about where you are today…the current reality as compared to the desired end state or vision. This type of thinking and comparison exposes gaps and opportunities for improvement to close the gap:

- Once you know what the opportunities are, you can develop strategies to close the gaps.
- Once you know the strategies, you can then allocate resources to execute the strategies.

Notice the sequence: *vision, strategies* and *resource allocation*. Without a clear vision or purpose, it is impossible to create the right strategies. Without the right strategies, how can you allocate resources correctly?

This idea is applicable at both the personal and organizational level. Creating a clear vision is important because your vision describes where you are going. It is a blueprint used by everyone involved in achieving the desired new result. The vision is about how you BE in the realized future.

Clarifying and sharing a vision is not a step all businesses take. In organizations, a 'clear vision' means everyone on the team has reached a mutual understanding or picture of the purpose and destination. This will take a concentrated effort, because people see, understand, picture, and describe a same goal in vastly different words and ways. Creating a clear vision requires that we hone the personal and team ability to see a new, better future. For some of us it means a 'snapshot' or 'a movie' we can see clearly in our minds. For others who are 'not visual' it might mean writing up in so many words a detailed description of the desired new future reality. Vision is essential, but so is how you communicate that vision. Clarifying sufficiently and in enough detail so that everyone is on the same page and headed in the same direction in the same timeframe is a critical first step.

Story Time

I'm not a big rugby fan, but the movie *Invictus* starring Matt Damon and Morgan Freeman caught my attention. It is the story of how Nelson Mandela (Freeman) uses the South African rugby team to unite a nation after years of apartheid. Mandela creates a vision of what a post-apartheid nation can look like. He uses the national rugby team, the Springboks, as a means to that end.

In the movie, Mandela paints a picture of what the future not only could, but will look like that is so compelling, an entire nation joins him in creating that future. Mandela explains the vision to Pienaar (Damon) and uses each meeting with him to coach, teach, and mentor. With skillful questioning, Mandela lets Pienaar come to his own conclusions about national unity and the role he can play getting others to follow him. He teaches Pienaar that the job of the leader is to get others to follow by influencing them, so they believe that they are capable of doing more than they think possible.

With the help of team captain Pienaar, Mandela succeeds in creating a new, united nation focused on renewal, reconciliation, and redemption.

Many lessons can be lifted from the story, but one is this: Leaders must not only create a vision for the future, but also communicate it relentlessly and then develop plans that turn the vision into reality.

Mandela himself said it this way, "Vision without action is just a dream; action without vision just passes the time; and vision with action can change the world."

Define & Develop Competency

This second KSA is about competency. Once you have a clear vision, picture or description of where you are going or what it is you aim to become (your future BE), you can then define and develop the right competencies needed to achieve the vision or end state.

Competencies refer to not only what your team knows and can do well, but what you the leader know, can do and can provide to them.

A transformational leader assesses his own and his team's individual and collective competency and holds it up against the clear, shared vision. You build an effective team when you have an eye on team and individual capabilities and know-how. This is where transformational leaders step up and go the extra mile with continuous training and development. Building the right competencies in teams also involves recruiting and hiring right. But it is from that base of abilities that you continuously evaluate and train with a focus on improvement, expertise, and increased skills that results in all those home runs.

You cannot disconnect effective personal and organizational leadership from change efforts or sustained Xcellence.

Once you understand the current reality—the requirements of your vision or goal as compared to the team's capabilities today—you can begin to close the performance or capabilities gap.

Building competencies and developing leaders is one of the top responsibilities of leaders. Not only is this the right thing to do, but the data suggests that leaders that have themselves been trained and developed with the right kinds of training, coaching, and job experiences outperform those that have not by 22%[3], measured in terms of executing business strategies. Those who are better at executing exhibit six of the ten leadership qualities of effective leaders identified by the researchers. This suggests that laser-focused training, coaching, and cross-disciplinary job experiences will also help increase the performance of every one of your team members. Train them.

Transformational leaders can learn from this axiom from professional sports: Coaches are known to tell multi-million-dollar professional players, "You get the big bucks by showing up for practice and training. You play on

---

[3] Source: Development Dimension International (DDI), consulting group whose core competency is leadership development and succession planning; https://www.ddiworld.com

Sunday for free." Xcellence doesn't take a day off, especially if you are aiming to achieve Xcellence and then sustain performance.

Story Time

Two small pieces of metal embossed with your name, blood type, and religious preference are standard issue items in the military. They are commonly known as 'dog tags' but are officially called identification tags. American troops first used identification tags during the Civil War when General Meade required his men to write their names and unit on a piece of paper that each soldier would keep with them or pinned on their uniform.

Some soldiers used small pieces of wood and carved their names into them. Paper and wood became round aluminum tags in 1906 and became mandatory wearable equipment in 1913. By World War II, the round design was replaced with rectangular tags. Every member of the military wears two dog tags: One on a long chain around the neck and one interlinked by a smaller chain. The purpose of doing this is so that one tag remains around the soldier's neck and one is used for identification in case of injury or death.

When I talked to groups of soldiers, I would often use my dog tags as a teaching point and begin the discussion by asking this simple question: "Do you have your dog tags on?" Of course they all had their dog tags on, at least physically. I would then discuss the use and meaning behind the dog tags and what it meant to "have your dog tags on". I'd explain that to have your dog tags on means you are a member of a team. It means you can be trusted and counted on to do your part. It means you live the warrior ethos.

The warrior ethos is a set of guiding principles by which every soldier lives. They apply to our professional and personal life and define soldiers in terms of who we really are and who we aspire to become.

The tags clarify the actions we take to make a difference:

- I will always place the mission first.
- I will never accept defeat.
- I will never quit.
- I will never leave a fallen comrade.

> Soldiers don't bunt!
>
> Making sure you have your dog tags on is a simple way to ensure you are modeling the right behaviors and leading a life of excellence. Effective leaders do more than master their own leadership skills. They always have an eye on their team. Great leaders don't bunt when it comes to supporting competency.

Competency and the Mendoza Line

The line between failure and success—or differently stated, between mediocrity and excellence—is so fine that we are often standing right on the line and do not know it. Many a man has thrown up his hands and given up at a time when a little more effort, a little more patience, would have achieved success. A little more effort may turn you from what seemed doomed to become a hopeless failure towards an excellent outcome. As Churchill once said, "*Success consists of going from failure to failure without loss of enthusiasm.*"

I did say that the Don't Bunt Rule of the Road wasn't about baseball. True. But let me make another baseball analogy, nonetheless.

Xcellence never takes a day off.

The 'Mendoza Line' is an expression that started in baseball several decades ago, taken from shortstop Mario Mendoza, whose poor batting average was taken to define the minimally accepted line of performance as it related to one's batting average for hitting. Popularized by ESPN announcer Chris Berman, the 'Mendoza Line' became a way to describe sub-par offensive players in major league baseball. "Mendoza usually struggled at bat and was known as a sub-.200 hitter whose average frequently fell into the .180 to .190 range during any particular year, even though his career average reached .215."

This 'batting average line' is often thought of as the offensive threshold: If you are not hitting *above* the Mendoza line, you don't even belong in the league. In other words, the 'Mendoza Line' is the minimally accepted standard of performance when it comes to a batting average.

At the personal level, each of us has minimally acceptable standards of performance. We tend to get anxious when we drop below that line. Your line might be different from mine, but they are nonetheless standards we watch on an individual basis.

Think about your organization and team. Is your standard of acceptable performance too low to get you to your stated new outcome? Keep in mind that this 'standard' may never have been voiced in so many words, but even so, everyone will gravitate downward to meet it!

Every leader on every team has their own Mendoza Line, verbalized and stated in so many words. Don't make anyone guess what the expectations *might be*. Tell them what the expectations *are*.

Your challenge is to develop competencies that enable a high-performing team to consistently play well above that line.

Building Confidence

As I develop the right competencies and execute consistently, I build confidence in myself, my team and other stakeholders. This third KSA of confidence is about boldness—not even considering bunting when you are up to bat, but swinging hard and true every time, because that is who you are and what you dare to do. Confidence is about swinging hard even if you should strike out or hit a foul ball.

The competency and capability you have built into yourself and your team members is the platform from which you confidently launch yourselves into Doing the things.

Here is an example of how competencies build confidence:

This military image painted by Rick Reeves is titled *These are My Credentials*. My Army War College class commissioned it as a gift to the college following our graduation in the Summer of 2000.

It is inspired by the surrender of German Lieutenant-General Herman Ramcke to American Brigadier-General Charles D.W. Canham, assistant division commander, 8th Infantry Division.

As you know, in the military rank matters...even with opposing forces. In this story, the German officer is a Lieutenant General (a three-star general, in other words) and the American General is a Brigadier-General (or one-star general). Three stars trump one.

As history tells the story, Canham faces Ramcke to demand his surrender. Not happy that he must surrender to a lower ranking American general, Ramcke addresses Canham through his interpreter saying, "I am to surrender to you. Let me see your credentials."

To answer that question, General Canham gives a brilliant response. He motions behind him to a group of battle-hardened American G.I.s filling the bunker's doorway, and replies, "These are my credentials."

That was an expression of pure confidence—self-confidence for Canham, certainly, but also a statement about the confidence he had in those soldiers he led. People are not only assets but are the ones that create value. He didn't bunt or back down. He swung hard.

Winning leaders and teams are those innovators who do bold thinking and take daring, results-focused action because they are confident. That kind of confidence only comes after skills, abilities and other competencies have been developed and tested in the fiery furnace of experience. They are confident in their own abilities and those of their teams. Being confident doesn't imply arrogance, but rather a quiet dignity, a quiet certainty, that your competencies have been developed and can be leveraged to deliver results. This can happen in many ways, but if you train up and trust the team to perform as trained, they will rise to your expectations and amaze you with their ingenuity and resourcefulness. Confident teams come out swinging as an everyday habit.

A Legacy of Xcellence

All business leaders should strive to create a legacy of Xcellence. Don't Bunt is a metaphor about being a focused, flexible leader who steps out and makes a difference. It is about action.

Don't Bunt means in order to achieve my BE or vision, I must DO something that moves me in the right direction…it means I am a DO-er. Not only am I ready to be bold but…I *am* bold. I have developed the right competencies and have the quiet confidence that my actions will deliver the intended result. I am not only working for success today but building a legacy of tomorrow.

Sustaining Xcellence is also about delivering your BE. It is about personal initiative and reaching your full potential and becoming better. Clearly articulating what that BE is, your personal or organizational vision, assessing the current reality so you can clearly see the gaps, and then developing the right competencies to close those gaps enables you to develop the confidence to consistently deliver results. Consistently excellence performance at the personal level comes from continual commitment to the goal. Modeling the right behaviors and creating a culture of action will allow your team to swing hard when they step up to the plate.

6 Rule of the Road #2: No Second Place Trophies

"No Second Place Trophies" is a simple metaphor for saying we strive for Xcellence in everything we do. It implies that I am focused on the things that matter most and not held hostage by the things that matter least. Johann von Goethe said it this way, "Things which matter most must never be at the mercy of things which matter least." In our personal lives, at home, at work, at play and in our communities and volunteer organizations, we always strive for Xcellence.

It doesn't mean we will achieve Xcellence every time. You won't. You won't get it right every time, and it doesn't mean we are not tolerant of mistakes and failures. But it does mean we have Xcellence as our aim, every single time we're at bat. We are always striving for Xcellence in all we do. No second place trophies.

With this Rule of the Road, we encourage failure faster so we can succeed sooner. We are always moving forward, learning, growing, and making a difference. It means I lead out from my strengths. I am a pioneer forging ahead—not a settler who is dug in, staying right where I am and accepting the status quo.

When there are strikeouts, you cannot wish away the outcome any more than you can change it. The real issue is how you react and handle those types of failures. If you punish or chide your teammates for swinging hard, it won't be long before bold thinking and action disappear. We must recognize that failing early often ensures success sooner. Likewise, every time you personally get up to the plate, you should be swinging hard. Set goals and objectives to stretch and test your mettle. But should you fail, treat yourself with the same respect with which you would treat others who fail. Learn and move on.

Leaders must always remember that people are led and things are managed. People produce results and are therefore our credentials, as we learned from the story of General Canham. In this light, you cannot let the fear of failure paralyze our pursuit of Xcellence. Second-best efforts will not do. You must finish what you start because as the slogan goes, "Beginners are many and enders are few...stick to the task 'till it sticks to you." The power of vision and striving for Xcellence will triumph today and overcome fear tomorrow. Developing a clear sense of purpose and direction is critical to becoming the kind of leader or organization you should be. When you develop strategies and prioritize effort and resources based on your direction or purpose, you ensure a unified effort and alignment.

What kind of legacy will you leave? What are you known for today?

Consider how Rule #2 No Second Place Trophies is all about a relentless mindset of and focus on Xcellence. It is tirelessly focusing on what I call your BFT, your 'Big First Thing'. That single focus allows you to consistently move the critical few forward and forget about the trivial many. You are being a pioneer, not a settler; you never give up on your personal pursuit of Xcellence, as Akhwari showed us all in this next story I share.

In 1968, a runner from the African country of Tanzania was sent to the Olympics held in Mexico City. The runner was John Stephen Akhwari and his event was the marathon: 26 miles, 385 yards. About 20 kilometers into the race, he was tripped and fell, injuring his knee and shoulder. Despite the pain and with no hopes of winning any of the three medals, he finished the race.

Limping to the finish line, Akhwari finished last—nearly two hours after the winner crossed the line. As he drew closer to the stadium where he would make his final lap, the stadium was packed with more and more fans watching this lone runner making the last turns and crossing the finish line. As he did, the crowd gave him the bigger cheer.

He was rushed by reporters and other media. When asked why he continued to run despite the pain and no hope of winning, Akhwari answered, "My country did not send me here to start the race, they sent me here to finish the race."

He knew he was accountable to his coach, fellow teammates and countryman, and most importantly accountable to a higher standard—the one he set himself. Even though he knew he would not be on the medals podium, he moved forward...slowly but steadily. A finisher.

For Akhwari, *not* finishing the race meant he didn't put forth his best effort. It meant he would not achieve Xcellence according to his own personal standards. Xcellence is not achieving the gold medal every time, although that is often one of the results, but it is indeed aiming for Xcellence every time you are at bat. Xcellence, like leadership, is personal, no matter who else you are accountable to.

Xcellence consists of the will to win and the will to succeed so that we reach our full potential. In this moment of decision and action, your paradigm of personal Xcellence matters.

In the end, the highest level of accountability starts with me…each of us is accountable to our self, and to our high personal standard of Xcellence.

I frequently see the idea of personal accountability in the office, at home, and in my community. All of these groups want Xcellence and strive to achieve that kind of performance by recognizing their strengths, setting goals, and working hard. They know crossing their personal finishing line is a worthy objective. I have also seen this attitude of Xcellence in the soldiers that have had the opportunity to serve and lead. This is one example:

Story Time

As a flag officer, you have the privilege of visiting many field and operations sites. You also have the honor of meeting with soldiers and their families across the globe. On one occasion, my wife, Carol and I had the chance to visit the Center for the Intrepid (CFI) at Brooke Army Medical Center (BAMC) at Fort Sam Houston, Texas.

BAMC is a Level I Trauma Center within the Department of Defense (DoD), and provides emergency services during 80,000 Emergency Room visits per year. The Center was created in 2005 and is funded with donations from over 600,000 Americans. The Center for the Intrepid provides rehabilitation for OIF/OEF casualties who have sustained amputation, burns, or functional limb loss. (OEF means Operation Enduring Freedom or the war in Afghanistan, while OIF stands for Operation Iraqi Freedom, or the War in Iraq.) It is a fantastic facility with a noble mission.

Following a welcoming ceremony where I offered a few encouraging remarks, we started our tour. We saw many soldiers who were beginning their long journey of rehabilitation and a return to some sense of normalcy. I was amazed at their attitudes and stories. I noticed a common theme: They always feel like they have disappointed their battle buddies and want to return to their unit. Amazing!

On the second floor, we passed a soldier in a wheelchair. His family, who was there for a visit with their hero, was pushing him along. As we passed, I stopped to say hello. I knelt down by the wheelchair so we could have a conversation. It was then that I discovered he was blind and had third-degree burns over 60% of his body...all the result of an IED explosion near Ramadi, Iraq. I put my hand on his so he would know I was there, and we started to chat about his family, his Military Occupational Specialty (MOS). We talked about his unit and the service he was getting at the CFI. He had nothing but glowing remarks about both. He made particular note of his family and how grateful he was for them. His mother and father glistened with joy. During the course of the conversation, he wanted to know who I was and what I did. I provided some generic answers that gave no clue as to my mission or rank. As we continued to talk, he kept asking about me...where I was born, my rank, and what I was doing there.

Finally, I acquiesced and told him my name and rank. Upon hearing this, he sat at attention and with great effort pushed himself up from his wheelchair. I tried to convince him that such an effort was not necessary, but he was having nothing of it. With a little help from his parents, he rendered a salute that I cannot and will not forget...ever. His crippled and burned hands were as straight as he could make them. You could tell that it was with some pain that he made the effort. I stood at attention and returned the salute. Then in a muffled voice he said, "Sir, when can I return to my unit?"

I think he could only know there was no chance of that happening, but I understood the sentiment and its expression. I put my arm around him and thanked him for his service and example. You cannot underestimate the power of purpose and mission, nor the faith required to deliver on your commitments of personal Xcellence.

There are no shortcuts to individual or organizational greatness. A price must be paid. We pay the price now by doing what is hard today. By so doing, we create tailwinds that allow us to do what is great tomorrow.

No Second Place Trophies is about moving forward. It is about never giving up. Ever.

In Support of Xcellence

The three **KSAs** (knowledge, skills, abilities) for Rule of the Road #2, No Second Place Trophies, are:

1. **S**elf-Awareness (develop a clear understanding of yourself)
2. **S**trength building (build on and play to your strengths)
3. **S**et goals (goals that help you DO, BE and BECOME better)

Aside from each of these tactics starting with the letter 'S', here is how I connect them. At the personal level, I am always striving to BE more self-aware and DO my best based on knowledge of my strengths. I am striving for Xcellence. The quality and nature of the goals I set will help get me to Xcellence (or cause me to fall short). Xcellence is the *only* level of achievement I am focused on or worthy of my energy, so setting 'stretch' goals is how I become and do better. As I build on my strengths, I am better positioned to envision the type of goals I can achieve that will make a difference and add value. My goals are tied to my purpose, and my priorities are aligned with my purpose. I must be able to say "no" to the seemingly urgent but unimportant distractions. During one of my many battle circulation trips, I dropped in on one of my logistical support units in Anbar province. Anbar province was known for two things: a radicalized enemy, and second, territory dominated by the Marines. Anbar was an important piece of ground because in the Fall of 2006, many Sunni leaders began to cooperate with the US and reject al-Qaeda. This change of heart was known as the "Anbar Awakening." These changes shifted the momentum from an insurgent stronghold to an area where the Marines and other forces were being more effective in securing the streets and protecting the people. Many argued that this shift was a model for other areas to follow. As we left the secure airport, I noticed a great sign. It read, "A Marine on duty has no friends." It reminded me of the seriousness of our mission and the impact that one Solider, or Marine, can have on the outcome. One of the responsibilities of leader is to ensure that the mission or purpose of the organization is clear and properly resourced. A singular focus is a combat multiplier in war and a market multiplier in business.

When I say "no" to things that don't matter, I increase my ability to successfully align my actions to my top priorities. I have a better sense of what would constitute a 'stretch' goal for me as I seek Xcellence.

Here is an example I experienced about thinking big and stretching for excellence:

Story Time

Risk management is an important area of concern and focus for any business. In one of the retail organizations I led, I was methodically working through all the key functional areas as we prepared our annual operating budget and report to the board of directors.

One area I zeroed in on was our risk management team. Under the umbrella of risk management, we included employee and customer safety, fraud, waste, abuse, and inventory control.

At the appointed time, I went to the conference room located where the risk management team worked. After some informal chit-chat, we dove into each area with a focus on the current baseline performance, goals for the new year that supported our overarching strategies and end state, milestones and accountabilities.

When it came time for the employee and customer safety team to discuss their strategies, they explained their current performance and goals for the coming year. Their goal was to decrease employee injuries by 5%. When I heard the planning number I remarked, "You have forgotten a zero". Confused, the team asked for clarification—assuring me they had done the math, reviewed the data and had the right strategies in place to achieve the planned reduction. I suggested that the target should be 50%, not 5%. They were stunned.

They expressed concern about such a major shift and, by and large, were unconvinced that a 50% reduction was achievable. I listened to their concerns closely to make sure I understood their point of view. We walked through the data again. We discussed the importance of safety and the financial impact of unsafe actions, not to mention the power of engagement. At the conclusion of the meeting, I challenged the team to think about the discussion—and then asked them to come back in two weeks to tell me what their current thinking was and what they decided to do.

They returned and laid out a plan to achieve the 50% reduction. This was a big breakthrough for the team, because they developed the plans to achieve the goal and were committed to owning the outcome.

Although I thought the reduction was feasible, I didn't want to 'force' a big, hairy goal on the team. I wanted them to own it. I didn't want this to be a 'me' conversation, but rather a 'we' conversation.

They also noted that they would need a specific set of skills and resources to achieve the goal. We also needed to realign and refine the KPIs. I committed to getting them the resources needed and, working with the HR team, made the KPI adjustments. We concluded this follow-up meeting by setting up a series of updates over the next year.

With the resources in place, the team started to execute, ultimately engaging the entire enterprise in the solution. Little by little, momentum was building, and we finally reached a tipping point in terms of a fully engaged team near the end of the first year. We didn't hit the 50% target, but we did achieve a near 40% reduction. Of course, the challenge with hitting big targets is sustaining that momentum year after year. By the time I left the organization, we'd passed the 50% target and more importantly, the programs became institutionalized as a way of doing business.

Building Self Awareness

When I say "no" to the things that don't matter, I increase my ability to successfully align my actions to my top priorities.

The core idea in No Second Place Trophies is that I work first on myself. If I am content with mediocre outcomes or effort, I cannot expect any accolades! If I am content with my personal status quo, and with resting on my laurels, I cannot expect that pat on the back.

In order for me to continually improve and reach my potential, I must have a clear understanding of who I really am—I must be self-aware. This first KSA asks me to have a clear picture of where I am (my BE, my strengths and weak aspects, behaviors, perspectives, values, ethics, and standards…) today as compared to where I want to go. I get a clear vision of the kind of leader I want to be compared to the one I am today. I must understand things as they really are. This process implies I focus first on myself or self-mastery.

By the way, using the word 'self-mastery' is a little bit of a misleading term because you never really master yourself. You (like most expert craftsmen, most profitable businesses, most copied mentors) are always learning, growing, developing, and changing in positive ways to move yourself. You are always 'becoming' a leader. Self-mastery is all about the journey, not a specific destination.

I understand my strengths and my weaknesses. I understand my opportunities and potentiality. From self-awareness and honesty, I see the gap between my actual performance or actions and where my stated personal vision is. All these statements apply to the team members I just told you about as well. They looked for and found their personal strengths, weaknesses, opportunities and potential—and brought them all to bear on achieving the goal.

When I begin to see the 'true' me, I recognize that I'm not as good as I think I am. That is not a trigger for anger at myself or for brow-beating my team or the world at large, but a trigger rather into humility…and more learning and reaching for self-awareness and Xcellence.

These 4 Rules of the Road intermesh and are interdependent. One way to build your self-awareness, strengths and set better goals that are tied to your purpose and priorities is revealed in the next Rule of the Road.

Strength Building: Play to Your Strengths

With a better and deeper understanding of who I really am, a picture begins to emerge of my strengths and weaknesses. This second KSA is about building your strengths.

Knowing my opportunities and strengths from honest introspection is the only way I can close the gaps between where I am and where I want to end up (BE). Knowing allows me to both mitigate my weaknesses and further build on my strengths. It is important to be aware of weaknesses; fixing weakness, however, only prevents failures or inefficiencies, while building strengths enables Xcellence. Playing to my strengths and allowing others to play to their strengths gives me the capacity I need to focus on my one BFT (Big First Thing). Leaders are always under pressure to deliver ever-better results. They are under the microscope to deliver strategies that enable growth and productivity and to do more with less.

Thus, one of the most important questions to answer is, "How do you stay focused on the task at hand while at the same time building capacity and capabilities for the future?" Maximizing talent is one way to ensure success now and in the future. Understanding and leveraging personal strengths is very important in personal growth, leadership development and sustaining Xcellence.

As leaders, we must identify and harness our unique strengths and allow others to do the same. As we leverage our strengths and build on them, we can reach our full potential.

The natural tendency is to dwell on our weaknesses. Such a focus is a good way to find 'work-arounds' to them or pivot them into assets. But it is also a way to get stuck spinning in personal criticism, low self-esteem, and despair. When we insist on focusing on our strengths instead, we are happier, more productive, and more apt to accept and even drive transformational change.

Our competencies form the basis for action and how we deliver results. Personal strengths are the skills we use in achieving goals. If we are truly committed to sustaining individual Xcellence, it will require change within us and our organizations along the way. It implies that we understand our personal strengths and opportunities and with that understanding we are in a good place to start the transformational journey.

Bestselling authors Tom Rath cited research conducted by Gallup in which over 10 million people worldwide were surveyed over a period of

Know your BFT.

a decade regarding the topic of employee engagement.[4] When asked if they agreed with this statement, "At work, I have the opportunity to do what I do best every day", only one-third strongly agreed with the statement.

33%? Really? Think of that: In most organizations, only one third of the team members have the chance to play to their strengths? As a leader, that gives me chills.

Rath goes on to explain that in a recent survey of more than 1,000 people who were asked the same question, among those who answered either 'strongly disagreed' or 'disagreed', he found that *not one person was emotionally engaged* in the business.

On the flip side, Rath suggested that people who have the opportunity to play to their strengths are six times (6X) more likely to be engaged in their jobs and three times as likely (3X) to report living an 'excellent' balanced life.

---

[4] Research in this section referencing employee engagement was comprised from the following articles:

Rath, T. & Clifton D.O. (2004). *The power of praise and recognition.* Retrieved from https://news.gallup.com/businessjournal/12157/power-prais-recognition.aspx

Rath, T. & Conchie, B. (2009). *What leaders want from followers. (J. Robinson, Interviewer).* Retrieved from https://news.gallup.com/businessjournal/113542/what-followers-want-from-leaders.aspx

Harter, J. (2018) *Employee engagement on the rise in the U.S.* Retrieved from https://news.gallup.com/poll/241649/employee-engagement-rise.aspx

An engaged team member is a person who has been given the opportunity to excel in what he naturally does best.

Consider this:

- If your manager primarily *ignores* you, the chances are about 40% that you will be actively *disengaged*.
- If your manager primarily focuses on your *weaknesses*, there is a 22% chance that you will actively *disengage*.
- If your manager focuses on your ***strengths***, there is a miniscule **1%** chance that you will be disengaged.

Those are startling data points and highlight the importance of playing to your strengths.

Story Time

Accepting the status quo is easy. It requires no emotional energy or intellectual curiosity to accept. You simply do.

As the Chief of Staff for the United States Army Reserve Command, one of my many responsibilities was to review and approve policies. You can imagine the number of policies, given a global force of 200,000 Soldiers.

Policies are important because they provide guidance. The purpose of policies and their supporting procedures is to explain what is required to achieve the desired outcome. An effective policy outlines the 'what' and the 'why' of something. If appropriate, the policy can also set direction, operating limits and define guiding principles. Policies are usually supported by procedures. The procedures answer the next two questions, which are 'how' and 'when'.

I reviewed hundreds of policies seeking to ensure that they still made sense and were actionable at the lowest levels of the organization. One policy paper I reviewed was focused on training and the role of the HR team in ensuring professional development plans were in place and followed.

As I read the policy, it struck me that it was outdated even though it was recently rewritten. It didn't seem to reflect the current reality, nor did it seem actionable. One thing you have to know about large staffs and action officers is that one of the objectives is to keep things moving, move the paper from your desk to someone else's. The mindset is "an action passed up the hierarchy is an action completed". This HR policy was clearly one that had been passed on without much critical thinking.

I asked the action officer to retrieve the related historical policies, including a copy of same policy. As it turned out, the exact policy was updated four years prior. I compared the same general policies that had been written over the past two decades. What did I discover? The policy updates were essentially the same. Sure, a few words and phrases were changed, like 'glad' instead of 'happy' and 'they' instead of 'we'. By and large though, no substantial or meaningful changes were implemented. The current 'updated' policy was no different—despite significant changes in the operating environment.

I used the opportunity to provide some coaching...we changed and updated the policy to something that made sense. The lesson: Do not accept the status quo because it is easy. Do the harder right instead of the easier wrong.

According to surveys and data, there are more than 22 million workers in the U.S. who are 'actively disengaged' in the organizations for which they work. It may take a leader and appropriate team members 2 or 3 hours to review a so-called legacy policy, but all-in engagement by functional staff and leaders is needed to make sure your ship is sailing under relevant rules. Disengagement is expensive: 'Employee disengagement' costs the U.S. economy about $300 billion every year in lost productivity. Sadly, these costs are not unique to the United States. But if you ask followers what they need from leaders, the clear answer is trust, compassion, stability, and hope.

We often deal with strength-building in our homes. Parents want only the best for their children. I am no different. How the 'best' manifests itself and the definition of 'best' differ from family to family, but I would suspect that there is near-universal consensus when it comes to schoolwork. I find myself doing what nearly every parent does when it comes to grades. Parents frequently think the student's lowest grade deserves the most attention and don't recognize the Xcellence shown in those good grades in any significant way. We often shrug it off as meeting expectations—instead of celebrating and recognizing great performance. Instead of investing *more* in areas where there are natural strengths and where there is potential for breakthroughs, we ignore them.

Playing to your strengths puts wind in your sails, builds on your competencies and gives you confidence to set goals of Xcellence.

Setting Goals: Spit in One Hand, Wish in the Other

With a clearly defined vision and a deep understanding of our strengths, you are in a much better position to set goals. This next KSA is about the much-vaunted ability to set great goals.

It makes no sense to develop and then set about executing specific goals (which I also call strategies) if the goals are not connected to your personal or organizational vision.

Many people (and organizations, if we are honest) feel as if we're adrift in the world, just reacting to outside forces rather than setting out to gain some measure of control over our destiny through consciously decided and focused actions. We all work hard, but we pause as we realize with despair that we don't seem to get anywhere worthwhile.

These Rules of the Road are a GPS taken as a whole; one other GPS embedded in them is the KSA of setting goals. A key reason people and organizations feel 'adrift' is that we haven't spent enough time thinking about what we want from life—what is important and how we see our life years down the road. Because of that lack, we haven't been able to set down in writing any relevant goals.

A 'relevant' goal is one that is clearly tied to your individual vision. You fail to realize that a goal not written down is only a wish. After all, would you set out on a major road trip with no real idea of your destination, with no clear vision of where you really want to go?

Goal setting is a powerful process for thinking strategically about your *ideal* future, and for setting objectives that are supported by very specific plans that can turn your vision into action and make your envisioned future a reality. Without a focused objective (your BFT) and specific actions, it is easy to get distracted. Setting goals that are bold *but specific* is the gateway to Xcellence and lays the foundational habits that determine our future. Priorities driven by a compelling purpose transform lives and organizations. F.M. Alexander said it this way, "People do not decide their futures, they decide their habits and their habits decide their futures."

As you set goals and achieve them, you also improve your competencies and confidence… your strengths and your engagement get stronger!

Here is an example of how to begin the process of setting goals and making the process part of your life rather than just a great idea that is short-lived. It is a simple process, but it requires action. As I tell my kids, "wish in one hand, spit in the other and see which one fills up first."

1. You clarify your vision—creating a picture of the future so compelling that at the personal level it ignites your internal fires and provides focus for your daily actions.
2. Recognize what you must DO to BE or BECOME the 'new' person you described in the vision step. This applies to both individuals and organizations.
3. Develop the strategies, plan or activities you must carry out—execute, perform, complete—to achieve your goals. Keep in mind that 'achieving your goal' is indeed your arrival at that newly envisioned future.

Change at the organizational level starts with WHY?, but at the personal level it starts with BE.

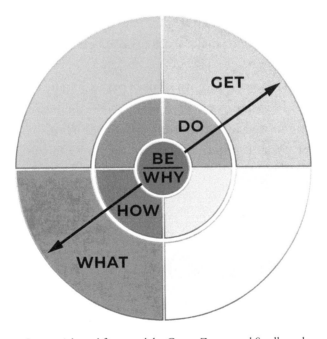

Source: Adopted from work by Covey, Zenger and Smallwood

This simple model highlights the importance of the starting point of effective leadership development. Once I am clear on my BE, I can DO. Doing means that I am confident, have strategies and tactics in place to achieve my stated vision, am all-in. To get clear at the personal level, the question I answer is, "What do I want to BE?" which is my personal vision. You must get this right and it is often a matter of working through several iterations until you get it right. You don't want to rework the vision statement frequently thereafter but remember that you are the author and owner of the document. What you create, you can change.

Break your end goal into small, time constrained supporting goals: You create a one-year plan, a six-month plan, and a one-month plan of progressively smaller goals that are nested and integrated. In other words, to achieve goal **C**, you must complete supporting goals **A** and **B**.

In response to questions I hear such as, "What goals should we set?" the answer is different for the individual goal-setter from the organizational goal-setters. You'll need to decide what specific goals are needed based on your personal vision. But one way to think about these is to establish a broad, balanced coverage of all the important areas in your life. Try to set goals in some of the following categories (or in other categories of your own that are important to you). Note: be clear on what it is you want to accomplish and then develop the supporting objectives. Once you know the gap between the current reality as compared to the end state, strategies become important to close the gap. Here are six areas that might make sense to consider:

- **Career**: What do you want to achieve professionally? What value can you create? How can you help others achieve their career aspirations? What do you need to DO or BE to achieve this?
- **Financial**: What is important to you and why? Do you have an earnings goal? How will you use your resources to add value and make a difference? What do you need to change (from your BE) to get the goal? What new action could you implement (from your DO) to propel you to goal achievement?
- **Education**: Is there any knowledge you want to acquire in particular? What information and skills will you need to have in order to achieve other goals? Are you interested in a higher academic degree? Where are you starting in relation to that end goal and what is your next step to getting to goal?

- **Family**: Do you want to be a parent? What are you teaching your family? How can you help other families? How do you define a 'family'? Do you have a role to play with your extended family? Do you want to leave your family a legacy?
- **Physical/Health**: What are you doing to facilitate a healthy lifestyle? Do you exercise frequently? What steps are you going to take to achieve such outcomes, given where you are starting today?
- **Spiritual/Personal/Later Years**: What other areas of your life are important and would benefit from reflection and thought or a new goal? What steps are involved in making those incremental changes?

One of my favorite stories about setting goals, persistence, and staying the course is the story of Daniel (Dan) Erwin Jansen.[5] Born in 1965, Dan was all Wisconsin. He became a speed skater, best known for winning an Olympic Gold Medal in his final race in the 1994 Winter Olympics after working through years of career losses heartache, and personal tragedies.

Becoming an Olympic Medalist is years in the making, as we all appreciate. His first Olympic Games were in 1984 in Sarajevo where he finished 16th in the 500 meters but came within a fraction of a second of taking home the Bronze Medal in the 1,000 meters. Dan kept at it and his competitive results improved by the next Games, having overcome a case of overcome a case of mononucleosis in 1987. In 1988, he became the World Sprint Champion.

By the times the 1988 Winter Olympics in Calgary rolled around, Jansen was a Gold Medal favorite for the 500 and 1,000 meter races. However, the day before the 500 meter, he was informed that his sister Jane was dying of leukemia. Only a few hours later he was told that his sister had died. He committed to competing based on his parent's urging. Emotionally drained, he started strong but fell early. A few days later in the 1,000 meter event, he began with record-breaking speed, but fell again. Despite being a favorite to win Gold, he left the 1988 Olympics with no medals, but became the recipient of the U.S. Olympic Spirit Award for his valiant efforts through tragedy. He went home to pursue Xcellence in his craft, in his sport, and for team USA.

---

[5] Dan Jansen's story was comprised from the following articles:

Dan Jansen. (2020). Retrieved from https://en.wikipedia.org/wiki/Dan_Jansen

History.com Editors. (2009). *Olympic speed skater Dan Jansen falls after sister dies.* Retrieved from https://www.history.com/this-day-in-history/olympic-speed-skater-jansen-falls-after-sister-dies

In the 1992 Winter Olympics, Jansen was again favored to a Gold Medal as he had earlier set a world record in the 500 meters event. But, he finished 4th in the 500 meters and 26th in the 1,000 meters, again leaving the Olympic Games with no medals.

Between the 1992 and 1994 Olympics, Jansen was the only skater to break 36 seconds in the 500 meters, doing so four times. In 1994, Jansen won his second World Sprint Championship title, and he arrived at the 1994 Winter Olympics for one final attempt at an Olympic medal.

In the 500 meter event, he finished a disappointing 8th. In preparation for the 1,000 meter event, he was coached by Peter Mueller, who had won the same event in the 1976 Winter Olympics. Well, Jansen defied expectations: He finished first, winning his first and only Olympic Medal of his career, while setting a new world record in the process.

He dedicated his Olympic Gold Medal to his late sister, then took one final victory lap around the rink with his one-year-old daughter, Jane. Jansen was chosen by his fellow Olympians to bear the U.S. flag at the closing ceremony of the 1994 Winter Olympics. For his efforts, Jansen was the recipient of the 1994 James E. Sullivan Award—presented annually every April since 1930 by the Amateur Athletic Union (AAU) to "the most outstanding amateur athlete in the United States". In 1995, he was elected to the Wisconsin Athletic Hall of Fame. Patient persistence pays personal premiums and long-lasting dividends.

7

Rule of the Road #3: Look for Yellow Cars

"**L**ook for Yellow Cars" is a simple metaphor for saying, "Pay attention to the whole of your world."

Have you ever been on a road trip with kids? If you have, you know they get restless and anxious. A common game on long road trips with children is a contest to either have them look for and count license plates from out-of-state cars or look for vehicles of a specific color. The point of the game is focus—seeing as many of those cars as they can and winning the game. They can't find those 'yellow cars' unless they are looking out of the car windows and 'paying attention' to everything they see on, up and down the highway.

The same kind of focus is needed for police or soldiers on surveillance duty. Like the kids playing the game, this kind of focus is not on a single point, but rather on a whole environment...they are always scanning the entire vicinity for activity and changes. Their success on the mission requires a wide-angle lens of attention along with a microscopic focus on the details that matter.

Beginners many, enders are few, stick to the job 'till it sticks to you.
—UNKNOWN

We operate in a small part of a bigger environment. And 'looking for yellow cars' is as much about focus on one specific thing as it is about widening the lens so you can observe the world from a broader context. We need to pay attention to the task at hand, certainly, while also keeping an eye on things in the broader environment. Effective leaders are able to pay attention to what's going on in their own team and industry as a whole, but recognize that regional, national and global trends impact their worldview and shape their thinking.

Extraordinary times call for extraordinary leaders.

This is particularly true in extraordinary times: Extraordinary times call for extraordinary leaders. In times of crisis, leaders come face to face with their leadership moment. In those moments, two things happen: 1) the character of the leader emerges (the character of a leader is not *developed* in a single moment) and 2) an opportunity is presented to that leader to refine or further develop (character can be *shaped* in a single moment) one's character. Those moments can indeed be defining and refining in terms of scope and impact, and be one of the foundational blocks upon which leaders build personal and professional resiliency. From this, they eventually draw strength and credibility. Leading in uncertain, volatile, and complex times is often the critical challenge that brings out the leader's best. Or not. Leadership, after all, has a lot more to do with who you are and what you do and rather little to do with any title, rank, or position. Without effective leadership, the only three things that naturally happen in organizations in extraordinary times are friction, confusion, and underperformance. As you look for yellow cars, your ability to lead will be magnified.

Story Time

During the early months of 2007, there was tremendous pressure from our US Congressional leaders to leave Iraq and get our soldiers home with haste. The war effort was considered a loss and a financial drain on the economy.

The IED (improvised explosive devise) was the weapon of choice by the extremists and the number of daily attacks was increasing, finally peaking at about 200 attacks a day in June of 2007.

During some of those dark days of my experience in Iraq, I was constantly reminded of the impact that leaders have on the lives of those they lead. Not every decision was life or death, but I think it's fair to say that every decision had an impact on somebody somewhere. The best decisions I made were almost always the result of looking and listening to my team...looking for yellow cars. I used this phrase (quite literally "Look for Yellow Cars") as a way to remind the soldiers in my charge to look, listen, and learn. To be observant of the big picture and to pay attention to the little details.

Why 'yellow cars'? The car of choice in Iraq at the time was the white pick up truck. Those white trucks were everywhere. They were used as the family go-to-market car, the business transport and—for those who would do us harm—the platform of preference for the mounted machine gun. So telling my soldiers to "look for yellow cars" was my way of saying that if you see something other than a white pick-up truck...if you see something that has changed, if you see something that seems out of place...it means the environment has changed. It was a reminder to pay attention because of this truth: The way you react to that change could save your life or the life of your battle-buddy.

To drive significant change in your life, you must change how you see things. Looking for yellow cars helps you see things as they really are. When you look for yellow cars in your life, you see opportunities and experience challenges. In those opportunities and challenging moments, you can sow the seeds of Xcellence.

As Stephen R. Covey said, "When I change the way I look at something, what I look at actually changes...if you want small changes, work on your behavior; if you want quantum-leap changes, work on your paradigms."

In Support of Excellence

Looking for Yellow Cars means that as I look and listen, I learn. These are thus the three KSAs for this Rule of the Road:

1. Look
2. Listen
3. Learn

Aside from each of these tactics starting with the letter 'L', here is how I connect them. My development as a leader—my personal and professional growth and improvement—is enabled and energized by looking for yellow cars. The idea of looking for yellow cars is a mandate to look at things from a perspective I would not ordinarily have—in essence, looking everywhere for out-of-state licenses on a monotonous trip down the highway, or for something that stands out as wrong in an environment of white trucks.

When you expand your thinking and how you view things, your perspective shifts. As your perspective changes, you are more likely to listen to others and see things differently…and you grow. New insights do not magically appear because you change your perspective, they must be developed through thoughtful action and thinking. When you strive to BE and DO your best, you are likewise growing as a leader. Growth implies that you are learning new things, considering new approaches and options, and leveraging new tools to help you understand other outlooks and perspectives, looking in new directions for better solutions. The simple sequence of looking for new things, listening with real intent and applying what you learn, not only shows that you are self-aware, but also has the secondary benefit of building collaborative relationships and empowering teams. Empowering others implies two important descriptors: responsibility and accountability. It also means that as a leader empowering teams, I trust them to make decisions, drive innovation, and pursue excellence that is consistent with their own values.

Your paradigms change as you open your ears to engage in active listening and open your eyes for active observation. Past paradigms shift as you look, listen, and learn.

Looking

We all look, but don't always see. Looking is the first KSA of this Rule of the Road.

Sometimes it is the small things that you notice that make a difference. Looking for yellow cars is a reminder to pay attention—to look around the corner so to speak. As Marcel Proust said, "The real voyage of discovery consists, not in seeking new landscapes, but in having new eyes." To view the world through new lenses is the essence of looking for new things.

When you Look for Yellow Cars, it doesn't matter what your IQ or street smarts 'score' is, or what kind of education you have received. You should recognize that every person and every circumstance is a potential teacher for you, and that sometimes it is the small things that matter. I learned the importance of this in following a call from one of my senior leaders.

Story Time

Sitting in my office one afternoon I received a phone call from Washington, D.C. Getting a call from the Pentagon wasn't that unusual, so I wasn't surprised. What did surprise me was who the call was from...the Chairman of the Joint Chiefs. And even more surprising than that was the subject of his call to me: AT&T calling cards for soldiers in the combat zone.

Although we were still engaged in active combat in 2008, it wasn't as hectic as what I call the bad years from late 2006 through mid-2007 when IEDs and the associated injuries and deaths peaked. At first, I thought the call was a joke. Why would the Chairman be calling me and why would he be concerned about AT&T calling cards in the middle of a major conflict? I scratched my head.

As it turned out, the Chairman was interested in the contract and costs associated with the calling cards. A week earlier he and his wife had attended a formal dinner at which a small business owner seated next to them and who sold calling cards whispered that he thought AT&T was charging way too much for the cards and there wasn't anything like the 'free' minutes AT&T was promising. In the spirit of ensuring our soldiers and families were getting the best deal possible, he wanted some answers.

He invited me to his office for a meeting a week later. In preparation for the meeting, I had several examples of the calling cards blown up (about the size of those checks you see that sweep stakes winners get when they are surprised at their doors) so we could see the details and fine print. At the appointed time, I dutifully showed up with my visual aids. I spent about 30 minutes with the Chairman explaining calling cards, pricing, limitations, advantages and disadvantages. He seemed satisfied that all was in order. I had one more meeting with his office on the calling card issue and responded to a few RFIs (requests for information), but then moved on to other issues. In the back of my mind, I thought the entire episode was a waste of time. I kept thinking, "Calling cards? In the middle of combat ... Come on, aren't there more important things to consider?"

My attitude changed when I was asked to go to Dover Air Force Base. Besides being the busiest and largest air freight terminal in the Department of Defense, Dover is the location where we receive and transfer the remains of the Fallen. These ceremonies for and with families are solemn occasions handled with dignity and respect. Every time I was a part of these ceremonies, I was reminded of how thankful we should all be for those who have given their last full measure.

While at Dover, I had the chance to visit with soldiers and families, as well as have a tour of the facility. At one point, we passed a small room where the personal effects of the Fallen were inventoried and secured. Glancing in, I noticed a set of AT&T calling cards, charred and crumpled. I wondered if the call had been made just before a mission. I thought of how that soldier may have used those cards to call home and what might have been said the last time they talked. And...I thought about my conversation with the Chairman. I thought especially about how wrong I was to think calling cards were a waste of time and an insignificant subject for a personage such as the Chairman, such a small thing to be concerned about...

Those calling cards certainly weren't 'a small thing' for that soldier. As I looked at those calling cards, I felt ashamed for taking my meeting with the Chairman so lightly. It was a stark reminder that everything has both a single and multifaceted purpose, and that everyone counts. We all stand for something and we all have a mission.

Let me tell you someone else's story to illustrate this point.

Looking at things differently—changing the angle, expanding the view—allows you to put things into a new, and often very useful, perspective. New perspectives can be meaningful as you seek to improve your life and the organization. Tom Rinaldi (2009), a reporter for ESPN and Lisa Fenn told this story (just one media report among many) about seeing things differently, in an interview of Dartanyon Crockett.

"As long as I can remember," Dartanyon said, "I've been carrying him from point A to B to C. Graduation was the first time I finally got to walk beside him." He paused. "It was a privilege. It was an honor." He was speaking about Leroy Sutton, a classmate and senior wrestler at Lincoln-West High School in Cleveland.

When Leroy was 11 years old, walking to school with his brother along the Wheeling and Lake Erie railroad tracks near his home in East Akron, Ohio, a freight train approached. Leroy got too close. His backpack got caught on one of the passing cars, and he was pulled beneath the wheels of the racing train.

"I didn't even look down," said Leroy, now 19, recalling the first moments afterward. "I was just staring at the sun the whole time. I wasn't trying to look down because that's when I would have panicked."

The paramedics who arrived within minutes saved Leroy's life, but the doctors could not save his entire body. At Children's Hospital in Akron, his left leg was amputated below the knee, his right leg below the hip.

He knew what had happened but didn't understand what he'd lost until a day later, when he lifted the sheets, and looked down.

In January 2008, midway through his junior year in high school, Leroy transferred to Lincoln-West High in Cleveland. By the time Leroy was a senior, he was a familiar sight (his wheelchair flying down the hallways) and a familiar sound (his laughter booming off the lockers). When he decided to join the wrestling team, just as he'd done at his previous school, the coaches welcomed him. They knew his story and were eager to tap his strength. "I told him, 'You've been hit by a train. What else—what kid, what wrestler—what can stop you?'" said his Lincoln-West coach Torrance Robinson.

Dartanyon Crockett was one of Lincoln-West's most powerful wrestlers, winning at several weight classes. At Leroy's first practice, his first partner was the only other wrestler on the team powerful enough to handle him: Dartanyon Crockett, Lincoln's best and strongest talent. He was 5-foot-10 with muscles bunched like walnuts, and already a winner in multiple weight classes. But when Leroy hopped off his chair and onto the wrestling mat, the competition was more than Dartanyon expected.

Hour after hour, month after month, practices connected them in ways that went beyond the gym. They went everywhere together: between classes, on team bus rides, at each other's houses. They dialed in together to a wavelength few others could hear.

"One day I'm coming out of my office," said Kyro Taylor, the school's power lifting coach. "I look over to the corner of the gym where the mats were at, and right up the steps I see Dartanyon with something on his back, and the closer I get, I'm like, 'Is that Leroy?' And it was Leroy on his back. Dartanyon's carrying him." It was not a onetime ride.

Dartanyon lifted Leroy onto his back and carried him to and from every match, on and off every bus, into and out of every gym, all season long. At more than 170 pounds, Leroy was not a light load. Dartanyon never cared, and the carrying never stopped.

"Most of the time we wouldn't get a wheelchair lift, so I would have to carry him on the bus, take his wheelchair apart, put it on the bus, then carry him off the bus," he said. "And then, into the building and up the stairs." Dartanyon lifted Leroy onto his back for the playing of every national anthem and carried him down the bleachers before each match.

Yet as inseparable as they were, a team unto themselves really, they also shared something greater than their sport. That's because the teammate who carried Leroy on his back all season long also knows about personal challenge: Dartanyon Crockett is legally blind. No puns, no jokes about their respective conditions were ever uttered between them. They were just two 'ordinary' but special friends, each one sharing his strengths and abilities with the other.

When I change the way I look at something, what I look at actually changes.

Listening is Not the Same as Hearing

We hear noise from wake-up to slumber; for the most part we are not *listening* to it, it's just background noise. Electronic noise, traffic noise, ringing, beeping and buzzing noise—it is the backdrop to our daily lives.

Listening to people with real intent is one of the keys to human interaction and is the second KSA for this Rule.

Not listening with intent results in comments like, *"He didn't hear a word I said,"* and *"He said he heard me, but he got it all twisted up."* Complaints like that simply mean the receiver is not actively, attentively listening to understand the meaning of the message, nor to acknowledge what was said.

Most of us have had some type of communication training. Sadly, most of that training is centered around expressional forms of communication like oral or writing skills. Very few of us had any significant training when it comes to listening or understanding.

There are many good definitions of listening, but I like this simple explanation. Listening is the "proactive ability to receive information and interpret that information so that the meaning and intent of the sender is understood". This should include non-verbal gestures or body language. Also, experts estimate that 60-80% of what we communicate and learn comes from what we see. That does not mean to minimize your listening! It explains why 'listening with your eyes' might be the most important thing you can do develop this important skill. In a McKinsey survey of nearly 3,000 change leaders asking what the most important leadership behavior was, listening was their answer. The importance of creating and communicating a compelling vision and purpose was the most important leadership behavior. They also noted that getting this right is the hardest leadership behavior to develop.

When you can correctly and fully explain with empathy what the other person has said, you are on the right path to truly listening. According to research regarding empathy, it is a habit that effective leaders can develop and nurture to improve the quality of their communication. What is empathy? Empathy is the ability to hear, understand, and share the words and feelings of another. As Roman Krznaric, writing for the Greater Good Science Center at UC Berkeley suggested, "It's the ability to step into the shoes of another person, aiming to understand their feelings and perspectives, and to use that understanding to guide our actions. That makes it different from kindness or pity. And don't confuse it with the Golden Rule, 'Do unto others as you would have them do unto you.'" As George Bernard Shaw pointed out, "Do not do unto others as you would have them do unto you—they might have different tastes."

Hearing is not the same as listening.

What are some things you can do to develop this skill? Referring back to the Greater Good Science Center, the Center suggested six habits you can develop to be a better listener, so let me paraphrase two of their ideas that are very powerful and support the ideas noted so far in the book:

1. Challenge prejudices and discover commonalities. Effective leaders challenge their own biases, prejudices, and conceptions by seeking to find common ground. They search for shared ideas and beliefs.
2. Try another person's life. You think ice climbing and hang-gliding are extreme sports? Try experiential empathy, the most challenging—and potentially rewarding—of them all. Highly empathic leaders expand their empathy by gaining direct experience of other people's lives, putting into practice the Native American proverb, "Walk a mile in another man's moccasins before you criticize him."

George Orwell is an inspiring model. After several years as a colonial police officer in British Burma in the 1920s, Orwell returned to Britain determined to discover what life was like for those living on the social margins. "I wanted to submerge myself, to get right down among the oppressed," he wrote. So he dressed up as a tramp with shabby shoes and coat, and lived on the streets of East London with beggars and vagabonds. The result, recorded in his book *'Down and Out in Paris and London'*, was a radical change in his beliefs, priorities, and relationships. He not only realized that homeless people are not 'drunken scoundrels', but he developed new friendships, shifted his views on inequality, and gathered some terrific literary material. He labeled it the greatest travel experience of his life. He realized that empathy doesn't just make you good—it's good for you, too.

Empathy is closely tied to the development of your emotional intelligence (EI). More on EI later, but for now we can describe it as the ability to understand and manage our emotions and the emotions of others. As you understand the importance of emotional intelligence you are better able to effectively listen to others. Learning to listen is the key to all effective communication and influence.

One reason this skill is hard to develop is that we have a natural bias to react and respond when we are communicating. In our attempts to show interest, our main concern is to respond in an intelligent manner and in a way that is consistent with the conversation. As we 'hear' the words, we already begin formulating our response. This is not active listening. That type of listening is just listening with intent to give your response, not with the intent to understand. Your focus should be on what is being said, how it is being said, all the while seeking to understand the what and the why of the conversation. Active listening implies that you are seeking to get a deep understanding of the other's point of view. Active listening means observing non-verbal cues to help you understand the words. To win in a VUCA world, leaders and organizations must be adaptive and agile and demonstrate a bias for action that is informed and fine -tuned by active listening and learning.

This is hard work, and one reason why in The Leadership Circle model, communication skills are among the first competencies to be discussed and fully developed after character traits. There is almost nothing as personal as those skills and nothing that identifies you better to your collaborators than your communicating skills—or lack thereof. Listening has a very powerful secondary impact. As I listen, I build trust, and trust is a critical element of radical collaboration.

Story Time

One of the activities I instituted was something I called my "Chaotic Communication Day." Two or three times a year I would set aside an entire day devoted to listening. Here is how it worked. I would invite the entire organization to share some thoughts with me on things that we could improve, things that we should eliminate, new business ideas and things that we should kill. The invitation went out to the entire global team. Anybody could participate and you didn't have to get permission from your boss. To keep the conversations focused, and to allow me to listen to as many team members as possible, we had two rules: First, you had 15 minutes to discuss your idea. Discussion was preferred, presentations optional. Second, this was not a sensing or complaint session, those types of issues would be handled in another forum. So, if you came with an idea you had to be prepared to offer some ideas on a solution and be willing to lead the effort or be part of team focused on the area you were interested in. You also agreed with the understanding that while your idea might be the "best thing since sliced bread," as seen through your lens, it may not fit into the larger strategy or resource plan...no hard feelings. Therefore, do not be disappointed if it doesn't make the cut. You could call, Zoom or show up in person. All appointments were on a first come, first serve basis. The calendar filled up quickly once the day was announced. For eight to ten hours I listened to as many folks as possible. I had someone taking notes and collecting any collateral information that may have been presented. The ideas and comments were then summarized and distributed for review. I paid special attention to ensure that those that had participated received a copy of the summary. There is nothing that destroys trust faster than committing to doing something and then not delivering. Ensuring that all the participants received a copy of the summary was a small way to build trust and to say, "I hear you, thanks for being engaged." I would often send the individual a shorthand written note or email thanking them for their insights. Once we received additional feedback, we then prioritized the ideas based on how they aligned with our strategies. If there was a new radical, but noteworthy idea or concept we adjusted our strategies to reflect the new learning. Prioritization was an important step because not all ideas are equal and most organizations never have the resources needed to execute every idea. We were also careful to keep everyone informed on the process and how their idea stacked up against other ideas and priorities. Over time the ideas that made the cut list were integrated into action plans supported by milestones and KPIs. Now, here is the important learning for me. Regardless whether the idea was actually implemented or not, allowing the team access to the senior leader, listening to their ideas, being influenced, getting to know them at a deeper level, provided psychological oxygen to the team and organization that formed one of the basic building blocks of trust and collaboration.

As you learn to listen, you are Looking for Yellow Cars. And, as you really listen with the intent to understand fully and exactly, you become vulnerable but influenceable. You cannot allow yourself to become distracted by whatever else may be going on around you, or by forming counter arguments that you'll make when the other person stops speaking. Nor can you allow yourself to get bored or lose focus on what the other person is saying. All of these contribute to a lack of listening, understanding, and learning. One other way to develop the skill of listening is to ask great questions. Asking killer questions is one way to find killer answers.

Learning

The best organization are learning organizations. The best leaders are learning leaders. The best teams are the ones that go back to the drawing board (analyze, research further, learn more) after a failure or mediocre result. You learn from others by both looking and listening. Learning is the third KSA for this Rule of the Road.

Every time you step out of your comfort zone, you learn something that will help you further develop new strengths and capacities. Likewise, organizations must be learning organizations and should be constantly building capacity for ongoing change. This emphasis on learning gets to the heart of the issues that individuals and large institutions are wrestling with today. It is not enough to change strategies, structures, and systems unless the thinking that produced those strategies, structures, and systems also changes.

Although, 'corporate training and development' programs had been around for decades, it was Peter Senge's 1990 book *The Fifth Discipline* that popularized the idea of the 'learning organization'. Senge suggested that learning organizations are those in which people continually expand their capacity to create innovative solutions and deliver Xcellent results. These are organizations where new and expansive patterns of thinking are nurtured, where collective aspiration is set free, and where people are continually learning to see the whole and to create the consciously designed new future in a collaborative way. The basic rationale for such organizations is that in situations of rapid change, only those that are flexible, adaptive, and productive will excel. A large part of that flexibility and adaptability is openness to do or try something new—to learn. Organizations need to discover how to tap people's commitment and capacity to learn at *all* levels.

Senge goes on to say the core of a learning organization's work is based upon five learning disciplines—lifelong programs of both personal and organizational learning and practice:

> *Defeating the status quo is the responsibility of leaders.*

1. Personal Mastery: individuals learn to expand their own personal capacity to create results.
2. Mental Models: individuals reflect upon, continually clarify, and improve their view of the world.
3. Shared Vision: leaders build a sense of commitment to a common end state.
4. Team Learning: developing critical thinking skills that enable teams to leverage collaborative competence.
5. Systems Thinking: a way of thinking about and a language for describing and understanding inter- and intrarelationships that enable transformative change and execution.

All of the themes Senge suggested are the same themes I have been outlining in the book. Organizations, like people, evolve, grow and mature over time. While all people have the capacity to learn, the structures in which they have to function are often not conducive to reflection and engagement. People may lack the tools and guiding ideas to make sense of the situations they face. Organizations that are continually expanding their capacity to create their future require a fundamental paradigm shift by leaders. This is one reason why leaders who defeat the status quo are needed. When you ask people about what it is like being part of a great team, they almost always suggest 'purpose' as the propelling force for action and trust as the glue that enables sustained performance. People talk about being part of something larger than themselves, of being connected, of being creative and innovative, and of serving with a purpose. I learned the importance of this on trip to Europe.

Story Time

Five years before the Berlin Wall fell, President Reagan commemorated the 40th anniversary of the invasion of Normandy on June 6, 1984. Standing in front of the 40-foot sculpted dagger symbolizing the soldiers of the 2nd Ranger Battalion, and addressing some of those heroes who were seated directly in front of him, President Reagan noted that, "It was here, at Pointe du Hoc, that the rescue of an enslaved Europe began."

Between June 6th-8th, the Rangers took the high ground scaling 100' cliffs to secure six German guns that were ensconced there...it was the toughest mission on D-Day. For two days, the 225 'Boys of Pointe du Hoc' fought their way up the cliffs and held the high ground until other Ranger units relieved them. By the time relief arrived, only 90 Rangers were mission capable. In this, one of his most memorable speeches, President Reagan went on to say, quoting from Stephen Spender's poem, "You are men who in your lives fought for life and left the vivid air signed with your honor."

Although I wasn't in attendance at his memorable speech in 1984, I had the chance to experience that kind of honor a few years ago. My wife and I planned a long-awaited trip to Normandy and invited my parents. We had been to Normandy before, but my parents, even though they are world travelers, had never seen the windswept beaches of Normandy— the ones that were code-named Omaha, Utah, Gold, Juno and Sword during operation Overlord. On that day, the Allies would suffer 10,000 casualties, and on Omaha Beach, 2,000 US troops were killed, wounded, or missing.

My dad is a Vietnam veteran with, notably, two tours of duty as a pilot. My grandfather had registered for the draft but never served. My brother is on active duty and leads the Army's hypersonic and directed energy program (he is also a pilot). Two of my oldest sons also served (one is a pilot, the other served in a Special Forces group). My youngest son is a microbiologist, and we are all members of the National Society of the Sons of the American Revolution. My two daughters are deeply patriotic.

Because my parents were turning 80, I was anxious to get them to this particular battleground of the greatest generation. After touring Normandy and standing on the cliffs of Pointe du Hoc, we visited the Normandy American Cemetery and Memorial in France. Located in Colleville-sur-Mer, the cemetery site covers 172 acres and contains the graves of 9,385 of our military dead, most of whom lost their lives in the D-Day landings and ensuing operations. On the Walls of the Missing are inscribed 1,557 names.

Just before five o'clock, I found my dad and wandered over to him. We both stood silently looking at the graves and thinking about our experience that day on the beaches and at Pointe du Hoc. I was humbled by the idea of such sacrifice.

As we both got lost in our thoughts, I got caught up thinking about Mr. Bill Mann as a young WWII private from the 112th Combat Engineer Battalion. I had met Bill some years earlier when I was the commander of a unit in his hometown. His WWII unit, the Combat Engineers, was one of the first to land on Omaha Beach in 1944. I again heard of Bill when I saw an interview Bill conducted with the local TV station in Waco, Texas. In this human-interest story, Bill described his personal duty to raise and lower the U.S. flag at the VA cemetery. He was a one-man honor guard... day in and day out, he did his duty.

I eventually tracked him down and called him on the phone. When I introduced myself as Lieutenant Colonel Keith Thurgood (at the time

I was the commander of a logistics battalion), he told me he had never spoken to a Colonel. I assured him that I had never spoken to anyone from the 112th Engineers. I asked him if he would be willing to come and speak to my soldiers about honor, duty, and courage. Like many from that generation, he was reluctant, but at my insistence, he relented. I was finally able to meet Bill personally, and I invited him to my office prior to speaking to our Soldiers. As he entered my office, he nervously snapped a salute. After some pleasantries, he began to tell me his experiences on Omaha Beach. He described the scene in the early morning hours as a time of 'anxious chaos'. His job was to place Bangalore torpedoes on the beach to clear obstacles for the follow-on forces and all the equipment that would secure a beachhead. Half of the men in his landing craft never made it to the beach ... either killed as the ramp came down or drowned in 15 feet of water. I cried as I listened. I thought, "Where do we get such men who answered their call to duty?"

After his talk with the soldiers, Bill later sent me a short note and a certificate thanking me for the opportunity. On the certificate, he wrote this: "At about 6:30 a.m. at daybreak, the 112th Engineer Combat Battalion were the first men to land on Omaha Beach in Normandy, France. Just as we reached the sandy beach, all hell broke loose. We were fired upon with everything—rifle, machine gun and heavy artillery fire. With the enemy fire so heavy, we had no choice but to head for the embankment. Some of us made it, but many did not. Within several hours the tanks, trucks and other equipment started to arrive. The slaughter of so many in such a short period was overwhelming. Even though many years have passed, I can still hear the crack of the gunfire, see the dead fall, and smell Omaha Beach."

As I stood at the American cemetery with my dad remembering Bill Mann, the names of the soldiers that had been killed in my unit while in Iraq flooded my mind. My concentration was broken by the sound of taps. I did not know this at the time, but each evening at 5 p.m., the cemetery plays taps. The standard military protocol when in uniform is to render a hand salute when taps is played; it is a small way we remember and honor the fallen. As soon as the music started to play, my dad snapped to attention, turned to face the American Flag and rendered a salute. I was still thinking about the graves and it took a few seconds for me to understand what was happening. I immediately joined him. Together we stood, silently saluting the flag and honoring those who had fallen on our behalf so many years ago. It reminded me that we honor those who serve by the lives we lead. Silence is a great teacher.

President Reagan's speech many years earlier concluded with remarks regarding Rudder's Rangers, who also landed on Omaha Beach that D-Day, "These are the heroes who helped end a war. Here, in this place where the West held together, let us make a vow to our dead. Let us show them by our actions that we understand what they died for. Let our actions say to them the words for which Matthew Ridgway listened: 'I will not fail thee nor forsake thee'". Who would have thought then that the actions of Rudder's Rangers—really just a handful of dedicated soldiers along with countless others who have paid the ultimate price, heroes all—would save the world? Let us take strength from their courageous action. Let our lives shine bright by the service we render; let that service 'sign the air with honor'. Let that service save the world again.

Where do we find such valiant men and women of courage and honor who do their duty? I have served with them and see them every day. Thanks Mom (she served too!). Thanks Dad!

You surely have your own 'war stories' that highlight the importance of looking for opportunities to change the way you see the world, and to start looking for yellow cars. But you can also change the world through one other simple shift in attitude and perspective, as illustrated by the 4th Rule of the Road.

8 Rule of the Road #4: Solve for Yes

Solve for Yes. This is a simple way of saying, "Be part of the solution". Welcome all potential options for solving problems or finding ways to adapt to shifts in the environment, and then implement those great solutions.

We have all been told no 'just because.' Government agencies, insurance companies, parents, people holding the money strings (you can name many more, I am sure) are notorious for saying 'no'. Usually, no rationale, reasoning, excuse, or explanation for saying 'no' is provided. I remember working with supply sergeants in the Army whose job it actually was to say 'no'. Don't get me wrong, there are times when it is totally appropriate to say 'no', and we want those responsible for spending taxpayer money to be frugal and conscientious, but can I please have a pencil?!

This attitude and perspective are unfortunate, but we see it and hear it every day. Hearing 'no' once is bad enough, but when it is the standard response to all queries and suggestions, it is a great way to lose customers and squelch a team member's engagement, motivation, creativity, and willingness to follow.

The world is full of naysayers and people who say no simply because they can. Often there is no good reason for it, but they happen to be in a position to say no and exercise their positional power to take the easy way out. People that say no for no good reason often lack the emotional energy, edge, or intellectual curiosity to move things along. Saying no is often easier because it doesn't require any extra intellectual, emotional, or physical energy. A no answer is the easy answer; it is lazy thinking in some cases. A no often protects the status quo and generally means less work for somebody. I've found that people say no and hide behind policies as justification.

They also say no because the reasons for *not* doing a thing are—for almost all humans—what pop up first in their minds. They see all the downsides, negative aspects, and disadvantages of doing the thing before any upside or advantage comes to mind at all. Common reasons for saying no include things like 'high cost,' a 'demand for additional resources,' or an unprecedented need for an 'immediate deployment.' The reasons for not doing a thing (solving that recurring problem; changing that failing manufacturing process; reallocating resources; repositioning soldiers to better support the strategy; etc.) are less intimidating and create less anxiety than doing the mental or logistical work of solving the matter with an innovative approach. Naysayers truly believe that solving for yes is more work and will even disrupt 'their' status quo—and naysayers are not comfortable with disruption. Fear of what the future might look like can be debilitating for many people.

Creating a mindset that naturally Solves for Yes requires work. You'll probably have to Swing Hard rather than Bunt. It requires you to Look for Yellow Cars. It requires you to seek out Xcellence rather than settle for second-best. It may even require you to take some risks and underwrite risks for your team.

Developing a paradigm of Solving for Yes won't be automatic, but a leader is solution-focused not problem-fixated. Solving for Yes means seeking to uncover real issues and their root causes. You do that by looking and listening. When you Solve for Yes, you engage the team and empower them to deliver results. You use the power of intent to describe what needs to be done and let them determine how best to achieve the outcomes.

Again, there may be times when 'no' is the right answer. But by and large, leaders actively strive to be part of the solution, and never tacitly accept being part of the problem. Leaders facilitate the search for great solutions. Great leaders learn to seek alternatives that are better than any single idea that they alone might have. This approach suggests that leaders are flexible and agile—and willing to accept change. Sometimes no is the answer because of long standing policy or historical traditions. Solving for Yes means making it easy and simple. Standardizing and improving processes improves performance and simultaneously makes it easy. My formula for success: Simple = executable = results.

Story Time

After I returned from my tour of duty in Iraq in the summer of 2007, I fully intended to return to my PepsiCo job where I led the strategy and innovation team. The Army had other plans for me. I was nominated for and eventually selected as the first US Army Reserve General Officer to lead the Army and Air Force Exchange Service, otherwise known as AAFES or the PX (the Post Exchange), and later rebranded as The Exchange.

Most people, even those inside the Department of Defense (DOD), don't understand that The Exchange is the DOD's $10 billion for-profit, multi-channel global retailer with operations in 30 countries, including Iraq and Afghanistan. The enterprise operates all the retail stores (brick and mortar), catalog sales, e-commerce and B2B activities, convenience stores, movie theaters, gas stations, name-brand fast food operations, manufacturing plants and on top of all that, operates a global supply chain network. It was a fun job and the only one I know of where you can be the CEO and a Commanding General of what is essentially a Fortune 200 Corporation.

In August of 2007, one of the Burger Kings we operated in Baghdad was struck by a series of mortar attacks. In the attacks, several of our employees were killed and others wounded. Standing in line that day was a young soldier waiting for his order. When the attack happened, he reacted like we expect all of our soldiers to react. Without direction whatsoever, he immediately started to aid the wounded and clean things up. This is one reason I love and honor the American Solider...they are humble in attitude, gracious in honor and laser-focused on the mission. When things calmed down several hours after the incident, this young soldier quietly left the Burger King and went back to his unit.

The next day, he and his fellow soldiers completed their assigned mission and returned back to the base. During their down time, this young American went back to the BK with his bloody receipt in his hand and approached the manager. At the counter he asked if he remembered him; the BK manager did not. The soldier reminded him that he was there during the attack and had helped clean things up and then said, showing the BK manager his receipt, "The thing is, I never got my hamburger...can I get it now?" And you know what the manager said to this great soldier? The manager said, "No, we have a policy!" Without further discussion, the solider simply said thanks and walked away.

I first got wind of this story when I read it in a newspaper article on a plane. My first thought was "No way!" We did not or could not do this as an organization. The article must be wrong or have the facts backward. So I took a big red marker, circled the headline and wrote a note to the COO with this statement: "Please tell me we didn't do this to this soldier." The COO did some investigation and sure enough, we did just as the article explained.

Now at first glance, you might be saying "that is simply, obviously and clearly a really bad policy". But, if you think about it, have you ever noticed how many old receipts there are lying around at a fast food location? The policy was put in place to preclude somebody from picking up an old receipt and saying they never got their burger. You may not agree with it, but from that point of view it makes a little more sense.

Once we gathered all the facts, I determined to make it right for this soldier. As it turned out, the soldier was home on leave. After I called the BK senior leadership and explained what happened they, too, were committed to right the wrong. After some coordination amongst us, we picked a date to visit the soldier as well as his mom and dad. We flew to his house, took him out to dinner at one of the local restaurants and presented him with a plaque to commemorate the event and most importantly, gave him enough coupons to supply him with BK for life!

Policies, procedures, and practices at the personal level or organizational level are not in and of themselves bad to have in place. However, if and when they don't make sense, we need to change them—especially if they keep us from solving for yes.

As you the leader learn to solve for yes, you begin to see the connections between people and activities. You learn to connect by looking and listening which helps you develop the attitude and skill of collaboration. When you collaborate, you create an environment that enables innovation and creativity which in turn opens the door for new and better solutions.

In Support of Solving for Yes

Solving for yes is a happy way to live! It is an energizing way to work!

Like the KSAs of the first three Rules of the Road, these next three tactics that you can use in solving for yes are about your personal leadership characteristics—your knowledge, skills and abilities that enable and drive action. The three for this Rule are:

1. **Connecting**—with people on your team and external stakeholders
2. **Collaborating**—across and up and down the organization and even across different enterprises
3. **Creating new and better solutions**—by putting all options on the table and selecting those that add value

As a trusted partner, you move into enabling team/organizational collaboration, and the natural result of deeper and more meaningful collaboration is a better solution.

Connection

Connection comes before real communication can happen.

Connection is emotional and personal. Connecting with people suggests that you are an empathic listener. What does that mean? I like this definition and it applies here: To be an empathic listener, listen with your eyes for feeling. I have also heard that connecting with people is "smiling with our heart". In both of these phrases you find the essence of connection…seeking to develop personal relationships that become enablers to Xcellence.

Nobody wins alone.

Connection is an exercise in viewing things from the other person's perspective. When you learn to walk a mile in their shoes, you gain a greater understanding of the lens (and filters) through which that person views the world. Your ability to connect is enhanced as you come to understand the importance of emotional intelligence or EI.

This idea of 'emotional' intelligence was developed based on the research of Daniel Goleman and suggests that EI is the ability to "understand and manage your own emotions, and those of the people around you". As your understanding or EI increases, you develop better awareness of how you and others are communicating, what emotions are surfacing, what those emotions mean and how they affect you and others. Goleman (and others since) suggested that leaders with a high EI are more likely to succeed and noted five key elements of EI. These people: possess high self-awareness; self-regulate; understand motivation; deploy empathy; possess good social skills.

My purpose in mentioning the importance of EI when it comes to connecting with people is not to make you an expert in the field (although why not?), but to highlight that EI, like leadership, is personal. It starts with your self-awareness and then you develop awareness of others and what makes them tick. You use that knowledge to build relationships of trust.

In the way we typically understand it, 'communicating' with one another has never been easier, due to our digital and remote tools: emailing, messaging, Facetiming, Facebooking, Tweeting, and voice mailing are the primary ways people connect these days, along with the business-centric video-conferencing, and the 'old school' phone calling. These are all means to an end, but not the end in and of themselves. They are tools to help us connect physically or visually, but not necessarily emotionally.

At the end of the day, I have a firm belief that those individuals, teams, and organizations that win in the future will be those that have learned to reach out and *connect* to collaborate at new and exciting levels. Collaboration, for organizations of Xcellence, will occur not just within teams but also across entirely different enterprises. That type of collaboration can leverage the global brain so that our thinking and interaction is improved and creative collaborative solutions to difficult problems to bubble to the surface. This implies that we have leaders that are not trying to protect their rice bowls, but leaders committed to defeating the status quo and rising up into Xcellence. Nobody wins alone.

When I was promoted to Brigadier General, I hosted a small gathering for a few friends and family. For each one in attendance I gave a small framed quote that I had written that said, "My life is a reflection of those that have influenced me." It was my way of saying that I fully recognized this achievement was not mine alone, but the result of years of coaching and mentoring by others. No one is self-made. Connect first and real communication follows.

Collaboration

Real collaboration, the second KSA with this Rule, starts with the connection I just spoke of. It then moves to you and me interacting at the individual level and ripples out from the two of us. This is one reason why I keep returning to how all leadership is personal first. If you are not trustworthy, collaboration is impossible.

The truth of rising through the ranks is that, as you move into more senior leadership roles, you have less direct control and more indirect influence. One way you can continue to influence is by creating a culture that allows people to 'speak truth to power'. Your people have a strong degree of comfort with who and how you are, and feel they can come to you with honest input without fear of painful consequences. As you do that consistently, your personal influence increases and you are able to collaborate and encourage collaboration at many new levels and with an ever-expanding number of individuals and groups. If you have the mindset of collaboration, your trustworthiness and influence will allow you to bring diverse teams together to solve the toughest problems.

Collaboration is easy to define but hard to enact. As a definition, collaboration is *'joining forces to achieve a shared objective'*. It is *'co + labor'* or laboring with others. It is bringing all the talents, skills, experiences, perspectives of the team together with purpose, to achieve Xcellence. A 'paradigm of collaboration' means you recognize that every single team member can contribute, regardless of their role or place on the organization chart. Everyone has the chance to be heard and to participate.

Because collaboration is about multiple talents, skills, and perspectives, you need teams to be comprised of people who bring those differences to the party. We call this 'diversity and inclusion'. It is important to call these two words out. It is one thing to have a diverse workforce that can be measured in terms of diversity; it is another to ensure they are included, each and every one, in the process of finding and executing solutions. Inclusion is a defined behavior that seeks to bring diverse points of views together. Diversity is much broader than ethnicity, age or gender, nationality. It is also about a team with a range of skillsets, life experiences, personality types and manners of thinking. It is about a group of people whose brains are not all 'wired' in the same way. That is where you get true innovative solutions for yes! When we tap into the deep reservoir of diverse and inclusive teams that collaborate, we always find new ways of solving problems.

Several years ago, James Tamm and Ronald Luyet published a book titled, *Radical Collaboration, Five Essential Skills to Overcome Defensiveness and Build Successful Relationships*. As the title suggests, they propose five key elements needed to build relationships of trust that enable radical collaboration:

intention, truthfulness, self-accountability, being self-aware, and problem solving. Note the focus on personal thinking. This is a different approach from a top-down command hierarchy. This approach to solving problems brings people together, engages them with a compelling mission or purpose, and then empowers them (gives them resources and tools) to deliver performance. These types of high-performing teams are responsive, responsible and accountable. Engagement and collaboration are personal, wherever in the hierarchy you are.[6]

Leaders that view challenges through the lens of a collaborative Solving for Yes seek alternative points of views from a variety of diverse sources. It isn't just about the top five performers or star players. It is leveraging the combined power of 'We/Us' to define the problem in various ways, so as to see the problem differently than one person might have at first. Then together, you craft an innovative (time-effective, profitable…whatever the need) solution that takes into account the best thinking.

Communication and Collaboration will win the day.

One of the primary reasons employee engagement is so low (by accounts I've cited, fully engaged employees represent less than 30% of the work force) is because we are literally not engaging them as leaders. An engaged workforce is a Solve for Yes workforce that strives for Xcellence day in and day out. Our best solutions emerge when we begin to see things differently.

Story Time

I was leading the Exchange, sitting in my office one day when I got a call from the Army G-4, who was the Chairman of the Board. He called regarding a card game. Yes, a card game. He wanted to know if I knew anything about a deck of playing cards called "Top Trumps, The Ultimate War Card Game" (no relation to the current president). I told him I had not heard of them.

The G-4 had recently had a conversation with the wife of the one of our allies' Chief of Army Staff. She was involved in some charities that were building much needed schools in Afghanistan. Part of their funding efforts included to market and sell playing cards at retail outlets and

[6] Source: '*Radical Collaboration: Five Essential Skills to Overcome Defensiveness and Build Successful Relationships*', book by James W. Tamm and Ronald J. Luyet, 2010

then collect a portion of the profit from each deck that was sold. She wanted to know if we could sell the playing cards in the Exchange and had asked the G-4 to investigate the possibility. She noted that she'd had ongoing conversations with some of the buyers at the Exchange but nothing was happening.

As I started to ask questions, I discovered that "Top Trumps" was a game that was based on the strength of various military units. Each unit was rated based on personnel strength, type of equipment, maneuverability, and other factors. For example, the 82nd Airborne Division was rated higher than the 1st Armored Division based on maneuverability (no offense to members of either unit). The higher the unit rating, the more likely you were to win a 'hand'. The objective was to play your cards, the ones with the highest point values, so as to win as many cards as possible...the one with the most cards wins.

I thought, "Why not?" But I needed more 'data'. You guessed it: I actually got a deck and played the game. After playing the game a few times, I could see why the buying team was reluctant to allocate precious retail space. (Seeing the problem differently, right?)

I reported back to the G-4 that the game was a bust...he agreed. But, as luck would have it, I was scheduled to make a trip to Europe and England and suggested that perhaps I could arrange a meeting with the Command and his wife to talk about the game and perhaps find a solution that would work for both parties.

Arrangements were made for the official 'office call'. Several weeks later, I was escorted into their personal quarters for lunch and a discussion. The lunch was delicious and the conversation polite. The outcome of the meeting was an agreement that the Exchange would purchase and market 10,000 decks and get them in our stores. We would monitor the sales and if there was demand, we would purchase more.

It was a good arrangement and we immediately set about to get the cards in the stores. I kept the General and his wife informed of sales on a weekly basis, but after several months we had only sold about 50 sets of cards...the buyers were right. We kept the cards on the shelf for a few more weeks and then decided to pull them. I sent a communique outlining our decision and thanked them for the opportunity to support a worthy effort.

Nothing else was said and we moved on to other projects. I forgot about effort until one day I got an email photo from General Petraeus and the Chief of Staff each holding an <u>unopened</u> deck of "Top Trumps". I had a smile on my face as I recalled that first phone call from the G-4 and was proud that we tried our best to Solve for Yes.

In that light, I'd light to share with you my super-secret formula for success. After you read this, you must rip the page out of this book and destroy it…This secret cannot be repeated outside the context of this book… Just kidding of course. Here it is:

$$E=MC^2$$

That's it. That is the secret formula for success. Let me explain. Most people recognize this formula—"E equals MC squared"—as one of the basic building blocks of physics developed by Albert Einstein in 1903 and which eventually led to other of his many theories of how the universe operates.

The basic idea expresses the equivalency of mass and energy. Stated another way, if you want to create a massive amount of energy (E), all you need to do is to take a very small amount of mass (M) and multiply it by the speed of light (C), squared (2).

Why do you get an astounding amount of energy? Because the speed of light (C) travels at 186,000 miles per second—669,600,000 miles per hour. In one year, light can travel a mind-boggling (unless you are a rocket scientist or astrophysicist) 5,865,696,000,000 miles.

So take a little bit of mass and multiple it by C squared and, BOOM! goes the dynamite. You get a big release of energy. You literally have an amount of energy that can change the world. Now I get that you are not an astrophysicist (nor am I), but a leader needing to accomplish many complex goals. Here is how I think about applying my secret formula:

- (**E**) = EVERYTHING that I do as a leader (engage, empower, energize enable, encourage, employee)
- is MADE better or MAGNIFIED = (**M**)
- when I apply the secret sauce of better COMMUNICATION and COLLABORATION = (**C²**)

When I do those things, I enable my team to take risks (Don't Bunt), strive for Xcellence (No Second Place Trophies), become a learning team and organization (Look for Yellow Cars) in order to always Solve for Yes.

$E=MC^2$ is a powerful formula for success. That's it!

Thus, at the personal level (you, your family) or organizational level (your company, your community organizations, etc.), if you want to create the massive release of human potential and fundamentally change the outcome, all you need to do is adapt the components of the formula to the issue at hand.

You can Solve for Yes when you learn to communicate and collaborate. Passing through this door allows you to connect with people differently and enables creative and innovative solutions.

Creating Solutions

Creating solutions that deliver value is not a once-in-awhile activity. It can't be. Otherwise you are missing opportunities for Xcellence. And therein lies the importance of this KSA—opportunities come to those who seek them. Creating value with innovative solutions is what great companies and leaders do, and they do it consistently.

The big challenges for organizations today are:

- What does my customer want? (And…Do we have it?)
- When do they want it? (And…Can we meet that deadline?)
- How do they want it delivered? (And…Are we equipped to do it that way?)

This challenge is exacerbated by periodic shifts in the marketplace and sea-changes in the trends of consumer expectations. Layer in IoT (the Internet of Things), big data, smart devices (and their mobility), personalization, market trends and just plain competitiveness, and you begin to see the need for a continuous Solve for Yes approach to solutions. You can't out-gun, out-maneuver or out-market all of your competitors. Leaders try. But we must play to our strengths and rely on our teams to develop new ideas and commercialize them as quickly as possible.

The types of solutions I'm talking about are not 'either/or' solutions. They are 'and' solutions. Solutions that deliver great value <u>and</u> an outstanding

Leaders are dealers in H.O.P.E. ...helping others perform exceptionally.
—UNKNOWN

customer experience. Solutions that deliver low pricing <u>and</u> great quality. Our challenge is to create a game-changing business model that leapfrogs the current trajectory <u>and</u> delivers significant points of difference.

You win when you are resolute about executing the right priorities, and when you remain passionate about employee engagement and operational Xcellence.

This supporting pillar of creating solutions suggests we need *everyday* greatness by:

- seeking improvements even when things 'work just fine'
- tweaking the efficiencies to drive incremental value to customers or to push down costs
- making things better for the guys and gals in the warehouse, so they can deliver faster or more accurately or more inexpensively
- improving the foxhole for the next soldier

Creative solutions are one way you Solve for Yes and sustain Xcellence.

Bringing It All Together

As a leader you are an influencer—connecting, collaborating, creating to deliver value.

It is your job to create an environment conducive to sustained Xcellence. For your team, it is an everyday Solve for Yes environment, where everyone knows that they will have a chance to participate in the process and influence the outcome. A culture of creativity and innovation means that you are always in the continuous improvement mode. To maintain a leadership position, an enterprise must foster a culture of innovation and change…keeping an eye on emerging industry trends (it's almost impossible to outperform the macro trends in any industry), leading change efforts or being a "fast follower." It means you realize there is always room to learn more, do more, become better, give better value, care more. This paradigm of continuous improvement is critical, even in, especially in, times when everything is going great. Why? Because the two biggest enemies of change are history and success. By taking action now, you are simultaneously preparing for an unknown future. You prepare now so your team is ready, willing, and able to drive innovation and make a change anytime a dramatic shift in the organization's direction is required to stay relevant. We all work together, kicking our collective and individual creativity up a notch, to create innovation solutions that win the moment and the future. Your connection with your team and their connection to each other is what, at the core, enables action and encourages a culture of collaboration and change.

As I connect with people and begin to develop relationships that help move agendas forward, I am more likely to collaborate with others. Collaborative relationships are built on the idea of mutual trust and respect.

I value people that are different. I see them as people of value that can make significant contributions to solutions. I bring together creative and results focused teams. I develop systems and processes that allow the power of people to flourish and to create the best solutions—none of which are 'my way' or 'your way', but rather 'our way'.

Our collaborative way allows synergies to develop that create new, better, more productive, happier solutions.

Story Time

The story of the 20th Maine provides an example of connecting and Solving for Yes...getting the job done despite overwhelmingly bad odds.

The 20th Maine Volunteer Infantry Regiment was a unit of Union forces during the American Civil War. It was most famous for its defense of Little Round Top at the Battle of Gettysburg. On July 2, 1863 the regiment, under the command of COL Joshua Chamberlain, was assigned a defensive position at the extreme left of the Union line. The unit arrived moments before the assault of Confederate soldiers under the command of Major General John Bell Hood. Despite being only fifty-percent strength, the men of the 20th Maine set up a hasty defensive position to repel the Confederate assaults. Outnumbered and exhausted, the 20th held the line for nearly two hours. Fending off repeated attacks from the Texans and Alabamans, the 20th Maine eventually ran out of ammunition.

In one final attempt to win the day, COL Chamberlain gave the command "Bayonets, Forward!" Leading the way, the exhausted soldiers followed. As one author noted, "Chamberlain's bold decision and courageous leadership led his men of Maine down the slopes of Little Round Top at Gettysburg, Pennsylvania and stopped the Confederate assault against the Union Army's left flank."

Now here is the background story as described by David Weart. "During the march from Maryland to Pennsylvania in the summer of 1863, Chamberlain's 20th Maine Regiment received over 120 mutineers from the 2nd Maine. These men had grievances with their command over their enlistment contracts and refused to fight. Given the orders to shoot any man who did not follow his command, Chamberlain faced his first significant leadership challenge as a newly minted commander for the regiment. Understanding the weight of the situation, Chamberlain relied on his sense of dignity for others and exercised disciplined disobedience in refusing to shoot the mutineers. In his speech to the men of the 2nd Maine, Chamberlain appealed to their needs and reminded them of the cause for which they enlisted. This moment served as a galvanizing force for the 20th Maine as Chamberlain's sensitivity and sense of responsibility strengthened the unit greatly. Influenced by Chamberlain's speech, all but 6 of the 120 men from the 2nd Maine joined the 20th's ranks and proved pivotal at the impending engagement on Little Round Top."

Chamberlain would go on to lead soldiers at other critical battles, including the siege of Petersburg, and was later awarded the Medal of Honor for the defense at Gettysburg. As a final act of honoring the great leader of character, General Grant asked Chamberlain to be present at the Confederate surrender at Appomattox Courthouse where he directed the Union Army soldiers to render honors as the Confederate soldiers laid down their weapons and flags.

COL Chamberlain won the respect and admiration of his men because he was able to see the value in people and connect with them personally. He was a respected leader because he modeled the right behaviors. He won the day because he led the way. The 20th Maine's action in holding the line has been credited with helping to turn the tide of the war. Sustaining Xcellence requires us to 'hold the line'.

9 What About Execution?

This book is really designed to help you mature your leadership style and philosophy so that you can teach others, serve others, and make a difference in your own life and work, have a great family, impact your community. That said, I wanted to add a little bit about execution and results at the organizational level…this may make more sense as you grow in your profession.

Leaders make a difference by executing strategies. Leaders that have been trained and developed with the right kinds of training and job experiences outperform those that do not, in terms of executing business strategies, by 22%.

This suggests that effective leaders demonstrate some common characteristics and competencies. Organizations engaged in long-term planning must give high priority to the development of their future leaders. Any organization intending to drive sustainable results and prosper in the global economy will undoubtedly spend a good amount of time and energy now to develop leaders who can lead the company tomorrow. Only by aligning the corporate strategy with the human capital management strategy will new leaders be prepared to meet new business challenges and compete in the global marketplace. Additionally, leadership development should be increasingly linked to experiences that occur within the context of work and human resource development frameworks. This will require critical, reflective thinking about how to synchronize the development agenda and it with the strategic objectives of the organization.

Many organizations are beginning to see and understand the important link between vision, strategy, and execution. Succession planning and continuous assessments of the impact of the leadership development process on individual behavioral changes and organizational success will also be critical.

Corporations are victims of less than stellar ROIs when it comes to human capital investments. American companies spend enormous amounts of money on employee training and education—$160 billion in the United States and close to $356 billion globally in 2015 alone—but they are not getting a good return on their investment.

Leaders today are faced with global challenges and must have the competence to manage the increasing diversity and rapid change. Leaders must be refined through the crucible of experience and then be given opportunities to leverage that experience in ways that fundamentally change the way organizations are led. Transformational change efforts always involve changing the behavior of individuals.

One of the most effective things leaders can do is to leverage the key components of change behavior by modeling the way. By leveraging an integrated deployment strategy, organizations can create an environment where change is seen as the primary means to deliver results, and where future leaders understand that character is the cornerstone of effective leadership and participate in the developmental process.

By "forcing" change, leaders may achieve a short-term gain and perceive what appears to be "change", when in reality sustainable change is driven by people. People must be influenced at the emotional level. Leaders do this by connecting character with results and by first focusing on themselves. The character of the leader is the cornerstone of effectiveness and bolsters the connection between results and effective leadership. Once this is clearly defined, the organization can design sustainable development and succession planning models. To the extent that such traits, characteristics, styles, and work experiences can be clearly defined and integrated into leadership development programs, including a robust succession planning process, leaders will be successful.

Effective leadership is centered on the character of the leader, the heart of which is personal trustworthiness or integrity. Effective leadership is developed from this core. The core forms the framework upon which all other behavioral traits hang. As such, development programs and supporting succession planning begin with a clear definition and an initial focus on *developing the character of the leader* as defined by the organization and its guiding principles. This is the first and most important step in leadership development and succession planning. Without the anchors of *trust and integrity*, the exigencies of public service drive leaders to behave in ways that destroy the trust of followers. Thus, contingency leaders will often encounter insurmountable obstacles on the road to leading change.

> ***Effective leadership is centered on the character of the leader, the heart of which is personal trustworthiness or integrity.***

Greatness, in the final analysis, is built on the foundation of individual worth and a fundamental self-awareness—a foundation centered on integrity, grounded in principles, focused on service, tempered with experience. The singularity and strength of the individual leader is at the same time the strength and weakness of high performing organizations.

At the end of the day, the credibility of the leader, which culminates in the *character* of the leader, is the cornerstone upon which sustainable performance and greatness is achieved. While the character of the leaders is of primal importance, the attributes and subsequent behaviors are only useful as they provide a bridge to achieve the desired results. This is why you must gain an understanding of these ideas and develop your own leadership philosophy and ideas…you must own them.

A trustworthy character is vital! Leaders are not gauged by personal traits and values alone, that is true, yet people will not execute for nor follow the lead of those they mistrust. Neither will they Swing Hard (Rule #1), Look for Yellow Cars (Rule #3), or Solve for Yes (Rule #4). Such teams, rudderless and leaderless, will settle for a Second Place Trophy (against all the tenets of Rule #2). A leader of character—a leader who is trustworthy, who acts with integrity, is consistent and congruent in what they say and do, who has a vision and is purpose driven is the kind of leader that will influence others to follow and deliver sustainable results. Effective leaders do more than master the key attributes of leadership; they connect their competencies, characteristics, and attributes with results. They are innovators that drive bold thinking and action. That is the type of leader that develops high performing teams that sustain Xcellence…it is the kind of leader we need now.

10 Supporting Models...Bringing It All Together

As I have attempted to demonstrate in these pages, execution is enabled if we have a framework from which to operate. This framework is based on two simple, yet powerful ideas. The first is that the models are integrated and underpinned by a common thread we call leadership.

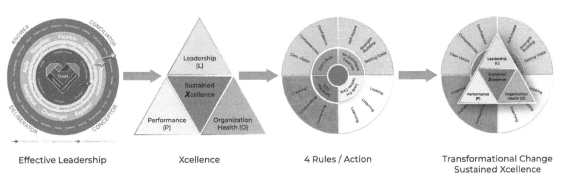

| Effective Leadership | Xcellence | 4 Rules / Action | Transformational Change Sustained Xcellence |

They build on each other, beginning first with leadership, because leaders at every level of the organization must make a difference. Effective personal leadership is the common thread and glue that binds the model together.

The second idea is that effective leadership is first and foremost about the character of the leader. The unifying thread that holds this together is trust. And trust is about becoming a person of Xcellence. It's about me; it is about my BEing.

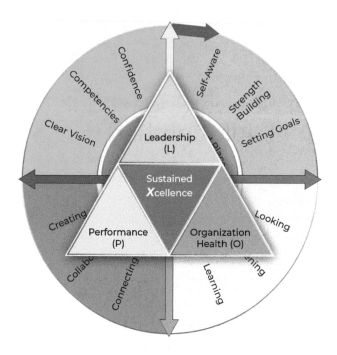

With a deep understanding of the importance of leadership, I can impact organizational Xcellence in the short and long term. More specifically, I can influence the performance and the health of the organization. Leaders have a defining, lasting, and multiplicative impact on both the results and the culture of the organization.

While it is important to understand the ideas intellectually and to connect with them emotionally, the real value is in execution…making a difference and adding value. To generate sustainable action, leaders must be clear on their intent, articulate a compelling vision and purpose, identify key supporting strategies and then align resources to execute. The *4 Rules of the Road* model takes the idea of leadership and sustained Xcellence and provides a framework to turn them into action.

In the *4 Rules* model, all of the elements of transformational change, at any level (personal, team or organization), are embedded in one of the three ideas: leadership, performance and organizational culture/health. Sustained excellence is driven by the interaction and combination of these three ideas and therefore are at the center of the model. Leadership, performance, and organizational / cultural health form the basic building blocks from which all sustainable results are derived. It's a matter of blending and leveraging the distinctions to make a difference.

See if you can see the key elements of the of the *X Factor, The Leadership Circle, the 4 Rules of the Road* and their supporting *KSAs* by identifying how they manifest themselves this next story.

Story Time

In late 2006, enemy activity in Iraq as measured in terms of improvised explosive devices (IED) was beginning to peak—approaching nearly 200 incidents per day. Consequently, deaths also peaked during this same time frame. Every unit was on high alert and focused on gathering and interpreting intelligence that might help reduce the impact of IEDs.

Late one evening, I received a phone call from the operations center that one of our field commanders had received credible information about a series of IEDs that had been planted along the main supply route leading from Kuwait to one of the forward operating bases in Iraq. I requested and received a detailed update on what was known and what was not known about the current situation. We poured over the intelligence reports and photographs of the area. We analyzed the route and mission requirements. We also reviewed the current supply inventories and requested shipments. After some 'war gaming' (a technique used to determine possible outcomes based on a series of decision criteria), I decided to stop all convoys until the route could be cleared and secured. Based on the mission load, supplies, and inventory on-hand and other priority commitments from the combat engineers, we estimated that we would cease convoy operations for 12-18 hours.

Think about that: High intensity combat operations. No resupply. Not an easy decision, but one I felt was necessary. The competency and operational insights of the team gave me the confidence to make this tough decision. At the end of the day, you cannot take shortcuts when it comes to sustaining excellence. Leveraging your competencies in ways to change the outcome requires leadership and bold decision-making.

On one occasion, we sent a convoy laden with supplies and equipment from Kuwait to Baghdad. The leader of the convoy was a middle-aged sergeant responsible for a mix of military trucks and civilian trucks that we had contracted for, and for a security detail. This was a normal configuration for a convoy heading North. Once the convoy commander receives the mission directive, usually in the form of a 'warning order' (this is an early notification that a formal tasking will be forthcoming and provides enough information to start the planning process; the warning order is usually followed by an 'operations order' which is an order to execute a mission), planning and preparation begins. Maps are reviewed, intelligence is updated, routes are reconnoitered, equipment is checked, and rehearsals are conducted. On the day of actual execution, one final briefing takes place that includes actions to be taken on contact with the enemy. This briefing is one more review that compliments earlier rehearsals and serves to reinforce key actions.

Several hours into the convoy, I received word that the convoy was under attack. Because the first reports in a combat situation are usually confusing at best and are at worst misleading or wrong (there is no intent to mislead or communicate wrong information, but in the fog of battle and intense confusion, it is often difficult to sort out truth from fiction), it was difficult to determine if things were going well or if we needed help. As the situation unfolded, the convoy was split. The front section of the convoy made it through the initial attack and was able to create a defensive perimeter and secure the supplies and equipment. However, the back half of the convoy was fighting its way through the ambush and was stuck on the main supply route.

As the reports continued to come in, the operations team began to take action to provide additional support and put the preplanned game plan into action. At one point in the battle, we got intel that many of the trucks carrying tanks and armored personnel carriers had been disabled. Fearing that the enemy would overrun the defensive perimeter and take control of the tanks, the convoy commander gave the order to get the tanks off the transport trailers and use them for protection and to enhance their fighting posture. Without hesitation, these magnificent soldiers took this bold action. They did not bunt! With rounds pinging off the trucks and hulls of the tanks, they started to decouple the tanks and position them for protection when help arrived. God Bless the Cavalry.

One of the things that is extremely hard to bear is hearing and seeing these types of things taking place in real time and not being able to influence the outcome. Look for Yellow Cars! In a real way, that is exactly what happens in large organizations. Once the vision is defined, key strategies developed and supporting plans are put in place, it is about execution at the lowest levels of the organization. That said, leaders must position themselves on the 'battlefield' to influence the outcome at critical points.

After the small engagement was over, the leaders began ensuring that all the people, equipment, and other supplies could be accounted for. As part of the equipment inspection, it was reported that in one truck, one helmet and blouse (the top part of the military uniform) was found. In other words, personal equipment present and accounted for, but no soldier... Not good. To make matters worse, no one had seen this soldier or in the fog of battle could remember anything about this soldier. As the reports flooded into headquarters, the immediate concern was for the safety and whereabouts of this soldier. Was the soldier wounded? Killed? Kidnapped? Or was there no issue at all?

In any such scenario, time is of the essence, and our efforts shifted immediately to gaining clarification on what was really happening on the ground.

After about 60 minutes of high anxiety with no clear answers, I was getting ready to notify the higher headquarters that we believed we had a missing soldier, a potential POW. Just as I was making the call to my boss, the operations officer ran into my office with news that they had found the missing soldier. I wanted confirmation. How did we know, and could it be verified? With a few more questions and some agonizing moments, we got confirmation that indeed the solider has been found. In the course of the battle, the truck had been disabled and the soldier ended up jumping into a truck with other soldiers, who had in the meantime made their way to a secure base.

When you hear news like this it is like having a teenage daughter who misses the midnight curfew and you can't get in touch with her to find out what the situation is. When she finally comes home, you are both relieved and angry. Relieved that everything is all right, but angry that she put you through that emotional roller coaster. That is how I felt about this soldier.

Transformational change—staying on the path of Xcellence—is not for the faint of heart or weak-kneed. If you are going to beat the 'whack-a-moles' of change down, you will need to be fully engaged—heart, head and hands. All in. All the time. Every day. While there are many leaders and styles, transformational change requires 'all in' leadership.

To achieve transformational change, you will need to continually work on developing the fundamental building blocks of effective leadership so that you can drive and sustain performance. Situations and styles may differ, but the basic building blocks remain the same and all leaders must grasp them… failure to grasp the *centering personal traits* of effective leadership will result in neither effective leadership development nor sustainable change management at the organizational level. That is why thinking deeply about your personal leadership characteristics and competencies and then developing a leadership philosophy and likewise recognizing that change always "starts with me" is so important. I will state it one last time: Without personal leadership, transformational change is impossible.

Now that we have come full circle, it should be no surprise that one of the key messages of this short book is that leaders make a difference at every level of the organization. Another recurring theme is that, as leaders, we must model the right behaviors and that those behaviors must be grounded on the basic ideas of integrity and trust.

None of us will learn all of these lessons or develop the three components of the **X Factor** overnight. Our own lives and organizations are too complex to think that a singular focus on any one aspect of the three components of the X factor framework without considering the other two just isn't realistic. We all know there are many variables that impact outcomes. That said, if you were to put an initial focus on one area, leaders and leadership development would be at the top of the list. There is enough empirical research to validate the impact of leaders on organizations. One example of this is research cited by Scott Keller and Bill Schaninger in their book *Beyond Performance 2.0*. They noted one 2016 study conducted by researchers Hartnell and Kinicki which found a positive relationship between the CEO and key measures like return on assets. They also noted that research conducted by McKinsey found that companies with leadership scores in the top quartile have a 59% of achieving "above-median" earnings.

But I have found that my own thinking and action is sharpened as I reflect on the elements of *The Leadership Circle* and my *4 Rules of the Road*. They have been and will remain my GPS as a father and spouse, a leader of soldiers, a leader of business teams of all types, a mentor and instructor to those I hope will be our Xcellent leaders of tomorrow.

11 Opportunities Abound

Leaders are more visible and more needed than ever before. Leadership of a commercial enterprise, or a military unit or any other organization is not a job, it is a calling.

Too many employees are disengaged from their work. With so many unengaged and dissatisfied people in the workforce, a leader has daily opportunities to make a difference by Being and Becoming a better leader, and by turning that disenfranchisement into creative excitement. Because, make no mistake, employee disengagement is on the leader. Mediocre performance is on the leader. A shaky vision, culture or strategy is on the leader. It starts with you.

Too many new and too many legacy companies fail to thrive, to weather the storms of economic and other shifts and to reach the potentials of Xcellence within them, because their individual leaders and collective leadership have not considered their own development needs first…they tend to believe the problem is 'out there' versus 'in here'.

In leadership roles such as the active military or in law enforcement, failed leadership costs lives. In commerce, failed leadership can cost entire towns and countless families their livelihoods and material security. Failed leadership in our education system holds countless numbers of children—generations of them—hostage and prevents them from maturing into productive members of their communities. Failed leadership in families leaves our children unprepared to make choices that matter. Failed leadership in our families has a generational impact on trust, accountability, and lost potential.

As a leader you are always being watched and mimicked. While there is not one single recipe for successful change efforts, what we do know is that change starts at the top of the organization—in and with its leadership. In a study conducted McKinsey in 2010 called 'What Successful Transformations Share', the authors noted three important practices to drive and sustain change (and all three are addressed in my models, albeit expressed somewhat differently):

1. *Leadership*. Modeling expected behaviors, developing the right KSAs (knowledge, skills and abilities) to build confidence; filling the leadership pipeline for organization longevity; and ensuring that the right team is in place to drive the change.

This last item can be particularity frustrating: Often the current leaders are the same leaders that brought the organization to a point of needing change in the first place! They are ego-invested in the status quo and many will not be supportive or see / accept the need for change.

2. *Engagement*. Communicating the 'Why' of change; creating a clear vision; connecting and collaborating within and across functional teams; and engaging stakeholders.

Engagement continues to be a topic of discussion and concern. Leaders struggle with how to motivate or engage team members. But the root of the problem is the leader, not the team. It starts with you, being passionate about the mission, about the transformations underway, about working with all the 'human' resources available to you and letting them clearly know that you and the team and the organization need their 'best self' every day.

3. *Accountability*. This implies that leaders create clearly define roles and responsibilities that enable everyone to play to their strengths. They seek a diverse and inclusive team that is constantly looking and listening for 'best' solutions among the alternatives.

Leaders can use a framework like the one I have described to drive action and execution. These ideas can be a roadmap and a guide for personal change as leader, a structure for action that enhances your organization's performance and as a way to sustain Xcellence. You can build on what I have described so that the ideas become your own.

Good is the enemy of great—and, as Collins suggested, that is one reason why we have so little that actually becomes great (Collins, 2001). Whether purchasing raw materials, negotiating contracts, or working through a difficult marketing proposition, leaders are at the core of the connected economy and are increasingly looked to as innovators that drive "great" business results. Greatness, in the final analysis, is built on the foundation of individual worth—a foundation that is centered on integrity; grounded in principles; focused on service and tempered with experience. The singularity and strength of the individual is at the same time the strength and weakness of high performing organizations. Nowhere is this truer or more important than in developing relationships with one's internal and external business partners. In the final analysis, the credibility of the leader, which Kouzes and Posner (1995) define as culminating in the character of the leader, is the cornerstone upon which sustainable performance and greatness is achieved. While the character of the leader is of primal importance, the attributes and subsequent behaviors are only useful as they provide a bridge to achieve the desired results. Results, after all, are what managers and leaders seek. It is the combination of results and character that makes an effective leader. This process is sequential and starts with a clear definition of what leaders should be and the characteristics they need to develop. Remember, leadership and change are personal. As you DO the right things and make the best choices at the personal level you BECOME a different and better person. The same thing applies to every team member and to every organization.

Story Time

East and West

I was on a business trip on November 9, 1989. I received a phone call from my wife excitedly telling me to turn on the television, exclaiming to me, "They are tearing down the wall." "What wall?" I asked, "What wall?" She replied in a pointed way, "The Berliner Mauer ... the Berlin Wall!"

To my surprise and amazement, I watched as thousands of East and West Berliners gathered at the wall near the famous Checkpoint Charlie, the Allies-manned Checkpoint permitting crossing between East and West Berlin. People were on top of the wall, hammering and chiseling at the wall that had stood as a physical and ideological barrier dividing Berlin since 1961.

Between 1961 and the fall of the Wall in 1989, over 100,000 people tried to escape the tyranny of the East by fleeing over the wall into West Berlin, but only around 5,000 were successful. That the wall was coming down was an exciting moment in history and for me personally.

As a young officer (this was more than two decades into the 'routine' of the Berlin Wall), I was assigned to Bremerhaven, Germany. In the midst of the Cold War, Europe was the center of action.

On occasion I had the opportunity to go to West Berlin which for me meant driving. To get to West Berlin required permission and a special pass that was printed in English, Russian, and German. Driving from Bremerhaven to West Berlin also required passing through two Allied checkpoints. The first, Checkpoint Alpha, was the border crossing at Helmstedt in former West Germany and Marienborn in former East Germany. At Checkpoint Alpha, I had to show my identification card, passports, and pass. I was given a security briefing and the mileage on my car was checked. Once I passed through the Allied checkpoint, I was permitted to proceed through the checkpoint on the West side to the East German checkpoint in Marienborn. From the East German guard post, I was directed to the Russian checkpoint. Once I was cleared from the Russian checkpoint, I was in East Germany proper and on my way to West Berlin.

Driving in East Germany was different from the Western sector. There were few cars, badly maintained roads, small villages to carefully drive through and an occasional gas station. During the 103 mile timed trip, I was not allowed to stop. I had 2 hours to make the trip, plus or minus 103 miles on the odometer. Rules of those days and those places were not to be messed with!

Checkpoint Bravo was the second Allied transition point. It was located near the Drewitz, a local community. At Checkpoint Bravo, the reverse happened. First the Soviet, then the East Germans and finally the Allied checkpoint guards vetted me and waved me on.

Although communicating with the guards was strictly forbidden, at each checkpoint with German and Russian guards, they'd use hand gestures to ask for cigarettes and chocolate, even an American magazine. (These items were rare if impossible to find in East Germany and either had great "Here, have an *American* cigarette" bragging rights or served as a way to make a lot of money on the black market from the items' resale.)

At Checkpoint Bravo, there was a time- and mileage-check followed by a security debrief. From there, after a sigh of relief and a huge release of a fair amount of stress, you entered West Berlin.

Getting into East Berlin from West Berlin required you to traverse through yet another checkpoint, Checkpoint Charlie. At Checkpoint Charlie, the crossing between the American and Russian sectors, I only checked in with the US Military Police. Once cleared, I would then drive through the Wall opening and barriers in a zigzag pattern. Once through the barriers, I was in East Berlin.

The contrast between the two 'countries' could not have been starker. You could immediately see the difference. In the East, nothing but gray, war torn buildings and old store fronts—all shabby with no thought of repairs. All shops had long lines of quiet people waiting to buy what few products would be on the shelves that day. Bookstores with German or Russian only books—all vetted by the authorities. State Security personnel stood watch on virtually every corner of the Eastern quiet streets...mostly pedestrians and some old streetcars, since few could afford the luxury of a car. In the West, the city was full of thriving businesses with lots of color, lights, and high design. Private cars were everywhere. People were going about their business so freely and happily, and a vibrant hustle-bustle to the nightlife in restaurants, cinemas, and clubs. East and West, night and day.

As I made those frequent trips, I would always ask myself, "Why such a difference between the 'two Berlins' and between the 'two Germanys'? Was it the political structure? A repressive government versus an open one? Radically different leadership strategies? An unusual code of moral behavior? No national / local foundations upon which to build a thriving, prosperous society? A combination of factors?"

As a young officer those observations and questions caused me to think deeply and critically about the impact of leadership and selfless service. Though my insights and understanding would mature over many years, it became clear to me that there is a code of moral behavior that forms the foundation of one's character and hence impacts leaders and their leadership style in every aspect of our lives: home, community, work, and the nation.

The Broken Bowl

For my birthday a few years ago, I received a special package from my mom and dad. I'm always happy to receive something from my parents and this was no exception.

The gift was packed in a medium sized box, and I knew immediately that my Dad had wrapped it (I would consider him an expert in packing and wrapping...he is a serious packer, a trait that skipped a generation and got passed on to the grand children). Not only can Dad pack a car trunk or moving van with more than twice the normal carrying capacity, but he is meticulous about packaging. Those packages are wrapped tighter than a rusted lug nut on a '57 Chevy...I'd recognize his signature 'wrap' anywhere.

When I opened the box, I was elated to see a beautiful walnut bowl that had been turned on the wood lathe. With encouragement from Mom, Dad is an excellent craftsman and works even the smallest details to perfection.

However, I was surprised and immediately drawn to the wood fragments that were strewn throughout the box. Large chunks and small pieces. How did that happen, given Dad's power wrapping prowess?

My first thought was that the bowl had somehow been broken in transit. My second was that I had better *not* tell my parents...especially Dad. He does not take kindly to mishandled mail where his projects are concerned. I know this because of the broken walnut bedpost from a few years back that was broken in transit. Much to the chagrin of my mom, he literally chased the truck driver down and wanted an explanation (but that's a story for another time).

In the end, I figured I would just gather up the pieces and put it back together, sand off the rough edges and call it good and then tell Mom and Dad what a great and beautiful gift is was. No harm, no foul.

As I started to gather up the broken pieces and put the jigsaw puzzle together, I noticed that a few of the pieces that were chipped appeared to have been glued back on the bowl already. What? I thought, "That doesn't make any sense." The thing is, it was the kind of glue job that I would do, definitely not something my Dad would settle for. It struck me as odd that the pieces would be glued on in such a haphazard way. Certainly not the kind of work I knew my Dad took pride in producing.

As I began to layer in the broken pieces I had in the box, I noticed more and more glue joints...all bad. As I looked closer at the bowl, I also noted it was not finished. It was surely smooth enough, but there were more than a few rough spots, and it did not have any type of finish on it.

And, when I put it on the table, I noticed that is was wobbly because the bottom wasn't flush.

By this time, I was curious about this 'gift' from Dad that was falling into the category of 'bizarre': A splintered bowl, unfinished, rough edges, large chunks missing, bad glue job... It didn't make any sense, and as I noted, certainly not the kind of work Mom would approve of nor Dad would do.

All that aside, I wondered what I would tell them and continued to try and put the pieces back together, eventually giving up for the day.

It finally dawned on me that perhaps the bowl hadn't really been broken in the mail at all. Maybe it was purposely sent to me this way. But, I pondered, who sends a broken bowl to their favorite son as a gift (OK, maybe not their favorite, but at least their oldest), and why? What was the story here?

A few days later I returned to the project, still with numerous questions rattling around in my head but committed to putting it back together. I wanted to tell my parents what a wonderful bowl it was, and how proud I was to have received such a wonderful gift that was handcrafted by Dad. I wanted to say that it was a beautiful keepsake to be admired and cherished for generations.

I had no intention of telling him that it had been broken and the glue job was terrible. It was to be, and remain, a beautiful, handmade walnut bowl from my parents, end of story.

Then, as I struggled to find just the right spot for the splinters and chunks, gluing each piece carefully in its spot (and mind you, my glue job wasn't that great, but I figured I could sand it down, fill the gaps and then stain it...an old woodworking trick), I noticed that Dad had written a note on the outside bottom of the bowl. In his hard-to-read writing he wrote this: "Happy birthday. 4 July 2018. Had a bad catch while turning, couldn't find all the flying pieces. This is the best I could do! It needs the touch of the Master's hand."

Finally, the pieces (no pun intended) of the story came together! The story of the bowl was solved.

Now, with perfect understanding, I could see what happened and why the bowl was the way the bowl was. I had new insights and a different perspective. I saw the bowl through a different lens. I understood the journey the bowl had been on, and why it was the way it was. In that instant it all made sense.

Like the bowl, we are all on a journey. We may be tossed to and fro; we have experiences that 'break' us; we look unfinished; we lived unbalanced lives; we have rough edges and a few smooth spots. Very often we try to put the pieces of lives back together, but it somehow doesn't look right—we look 'chipped-away-at' or frazzled. And, from our inward-looking perspective, the pieces just don't seem to fit.

We have a natural tendency to view ourselves through the mirror of worldly reflection…in a way we think others view us. Our value is often determined by how we see ourselves, not when we look in the mirror, but in relation to others. We see ourselves as never quite good enough and are hindered by our self-judgment. Nevertheless, there are some lessons to be learned.

1. It isn't always the mail.

There is a natural tendency to blame others, the environment, circumstances, industry trends, or society for our lives and the associated outcomes. As has often been said, we will all drink out of some bitter cups. The question is, will we become better or remain bitter?

We must take responsibility. Things usually work out best if you make the best out of the way things turn out. Own it…lean in…be comfortable in the uncomfortable. Our heart beats 100,000 times a day, 36 million times each year. Make every moment matter.

Questions to consider: Do I accept responsibility for my actions? Do I make great choices? Do I believe that all these things are for my experience? Do I make the best of every situation?

2. We all have our rough edges.

Scott Peck, author of *The Road Less Traveled*, noted that it is in this world of meeting and solving problems that life has meaning. Problems, he said, are the cutting edge that distinguishes between success and failure.

Problems call forth our courage and wisdom; indeed they create our courage and our wisdom. It is only because of problems that we grow emotionally, mentally, socially and spiritually. It is through pain of confronting and resolving problems that we learn. Sometimes it is the very things that hurt, that also instruct and edify.

> Questions to consider: What lessons have I learned? Am I grateful for this experience? How has this experience refined me and softened my edges? Where do I go from here?

3. Recognize your potential and play to your strengths.

I like what Marianne Williamson said, "Our deepest fear is not that we are inadequate. Our deepest fear is that we are powerful beyond measure. It is our light, not our darkness, that most frightens us."

You and I are included in this statement by C.S. Lewis, "There are no ordinary people. You have never talked to a mere mortal. Nations, cultures, arts, civilizations—these are mortal, and their life is to ours as the life of a gnat. But it is immortals whom we joke with, work with, marry, snub and exploit—immortal horrors or everlasting splendors. This does not mean that we are to be perpetually solemn. We must play. But our merriment must be of that kind (and it is, in fact, the merriest kind) which exists between people who have, from the outset, taken each other seriously—no flippancy, no superiority, no presumption."

> Questions to Consider: Do I see myself as a person of potential? Do I recognize the royal in me? Where do I need development? What do I want out of life? How do I develop the right knowledge, skills and attributes?

4. Fail Forward.

Growth is always a matter of choice, never a matter of chance. We are called upon to endure hard things. In fact, the word '*endure*' comes from the Latin root, '*durare*', which means to last, to be strong, or to become hard.

Johann Wolfgang von Goethe said that, "Thinking is easy, acting is difficult, and to put one's thoughts into action is the most difficult thing in the world."

Gail Sheehy had similar sentiments, "If we don't change, we don't grow. If we don't grow, we are not really living. Growth demands a temporary surrender of security. It may mean giving up of familiar but limiting patterns."

Henry Ward Beecher, "It is defeat that turns bone to flint, and gristle to muscle, and makes people invincible, and formed those heroic natures that are not in ascendancy in the world. Do not, then, be afraid of defeat. You are never so near to victory as when defeated in a good cause."

> Questions to consider: Where am I now? Am I where I want to be? What is the gap between my "best" self or destination? What is my dream? What is my plan to close the gap?

Well, then, with the bowl mystery solved, I decided to call my parents and thank them for the bowl, pieces and all, but most importantly for the message. As I told the story to my mom and dad, and how I eventually came to realize what the gift was, we all had a big chuckle. They were sure I could use the bowl as an object lesson in one of my many classes or teaching moments. They were right. The biggest teaching moments are mine to learn.

The journey of **developing your personal leadership capabilities** using some of the ideas in the preceding pages will serve you in all aspects of your life. Leadership is needed in business, have no doubt. We will always need great leaders and followers. We need leaders to come together to improve our communities and society at large. We need great leaders to lead the nation, and perhaps most importantly we need great leaders to teach our children and extended families so that they too can make a difference and leave a legacy of excellence. Thus, to reverse that popular saying which says that "It's not personal; it's business!"—leadership is not just business, *but it is always personal.*

But, like my observations and insights about the broken bowl, sometimes we only see how the pieces fit together and recognize the value of our experiences with perfect 20-20 hindsight. We tend to look at ourselves as we are, not as the type of leader we can and should become. The French writer Charles Du Bos said it this way, "The important thing is this: To be able at any moment to sacrifice what we are for what we could become."

This is the journey of personal leadership.

What I've Learned

My 4 Rules of the Road and the 12 KSAs

Here again are my Rules of the Road with their corresponding Knowledge, Skills and Abilities.

1. Don't Bunt

    a) **C**larify vision
    b) Define **C**ompetencies
    c) Build **C**onfidence

2. No Second Place Trophies

    a) **S**elf-awareness—be a self-aware leader
    b) **S**trength building / playing to your strengths
    c) **S**et goals that help you do and become better

3. Look for Yellow Cars

    a) **L**ook for things that you would not ordinarily look for
    b) **L**isten to everyone
    c) **L**earn continuously

4. Solve for Yes

    a) **C**onnect with people
    b) **C**ollaborate broadly
    c) **C**reate new and better solutions

References
And Other Publications That Might be Helpful

Bennis, W. (1989). *On becoming a leader.* Wilmington, MA: Perseus Books Group.

Bennis, W. & Goldsmith, J. (1997). *Learning to lead.* Cambridge, MA: Perseus Books.

Bennis, W. & Thomas, R. (2002). *Geeks and geezers.* Boston, MA. Harvard Business School Press.

Burns, J. (1978). *Leadership.* New York: Harper & Row.

Collins, J. (2001). *Good to great: Why some companies make the leap and others don't.* New York: Harper Collins.

Covey, S. (1990). *Principle-centered leadership.* Provo, Utah: The Institute for Principle-Centered Leadership, Publishers.

DePree, M. (1989). *Leadership is an art.* New York: Doubleday.

Fister, D. (2002). *Change management: Ready, set, go.* New York: Random House.

Goleman, D. (2000, March-April). Leadership that gets results. *Harvard Business Review.*

Harter, J. (2018) *Employee engagement on the rise in the U.S.* Retrieved from https://news.gallup.com/poll/241649/employee-engagement-rise.aspx

Heifetz, R. & Laurie, D. (1997, Jan-Feb). The work of leadership. *Harvard Business Review*

Hesselbein, F., Goldsmith, M., & Beckhard, R. (1996). *The leader of the future by the drucker foundation.* San Francisco: Jossey-Bass Publishers.

Keller, S., & Price, C. (2011). *Beyond performance: How great organizations build ultimate competitive advantage.* Hoboken, NJ: John Wiley & Sons.

Kellerman, B. (2004). Leadership: warts and all. *Harvard Business Review*, January, 10-45.

Kotter, J. P. (1996). *Leading change*. Boston: Harvard Business School Press.

Kouzes, J. M., & Posner, B. Z. (1995). *The leadership challenge: How to keep getting extraordinary things done in organizations* (2nd ed.). San Francisco, CA: Jossey-Bass Publishers.

McCall, M., Lombardo, M., & Morrison, A. (1998). *The lessons of experience: How successful executives develop on the job*. New York: The Free Press.

McGregor-Burns, J. (1978). *Leadership*. New York: Harper & Row.

Miller, M. (1997). *Brainstyles: Change your life without changing who you are*. New York: Simon & Schuster.

O'Toole, J. (1995). *Leading change, the argument for values-based leadership*. San Francisco: Jossey-Bass Inc., Publishers.

Peters, T. & Waterman, R. (1982). *In search of excellence*. New York: Harper & Row.

Puryear, E. (2000). *American generalship, character is everything*. Novato, CA: Presidio Press.

Rath, T. & Clifton D.O. (2004). *The power of praise and recognition*. Retrieved from https://news.gallup.com/businessjournal/12157/power-prais-recognition.aspx

Rath, T. & Conchie, B. (2009). *What leaders want from followers*. (J. Robinson, Interviewer). Retrieved from https://news.gallup.com/businessjournal/113542/what-followers-want-from-leaders.aspx

Rinaldi, T. & Fenn, L. (2009). *High school teammates carry on*. Retrieved from https://www.espn.com/espn/otl/news/story?id=4371874

Senge, P. (1990) *The fifth discipline*. New York: Doubleday Books

Tead, O. (1935). *The art of leadership*. New York: McGraw-Hill Book Co., Inc.

Tichy, N. M., & Devanna, M. A. (1986). *The transformational leader*. New York: Wiley Publishers.

Useem, M. (1998). *The leadership moment*. New York: Time Books.

Ulrich D., Zenger J. & Smallwood, N. (1999). *Results-based leadership*. Boston: Harvard Business School Press.

Vicere, A. A., & Fulmer, R. M. (1997). *Leadership development by design*. Boston: Harvard Business School Press.

Zand, D. E. (1997). *The leadership triad: Knowledge, trust, and power*. New York: Oxford University Press.

Appendix
Other Ideas That You Might Find Helpful

Change Leader Practices

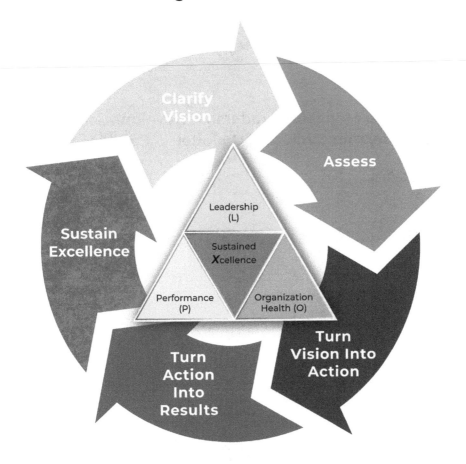

The Change Model:
5 Building Blocks and 20

3D Model for Leadership Development
The Leadership Circle . . . 3D Model . . . Food for Thought

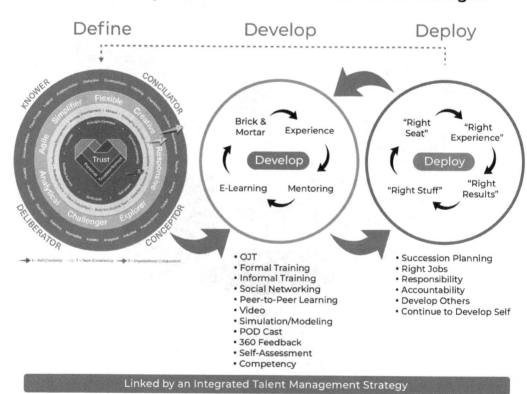

Index

About the Author
Keith L. Thurgood, Ph.D.

Keith Thurgood is currently a Clinical Professor of Healthcare Leadership and Management at the University of Texas Dallas's Jindal School of Management. He also leads the graduate program in Healthcare Leadership and Management and is an Adjunct Professor of Marketing and Entrepreneurship. In addition to his responsibilities at UT Dallas, Dr. Thurgood is a faculty member and senior advisor for the Thayer Leader Development Group (West Point, New York).

Dr. Thurgood was President of MedAssets Spend and Clinical Resource Management, a healthcare performance improvement company. He served as President and CEO of Overseas Military Sales Corporation and as the Senior Vice President of Operations for Sam's Club. He was also the CEO of the Army and Air Force Exchange Service, the Department of Defense's $10B for-profit retail organization. He has held executive positions with both Frito-Lay and PepsiCo.

Dr. Thurgood recently returned to UTD following a 14-month sabbatical he took after an appointment by the Secretary of Defense Chief Management Officer to lead the largest global community services, retail, and grocery reform effort in a generation.

In addition to his civilian corporate and academic work, he has over 28 years of Army service, both active and reserve. Major General Thurgood served simultaneously as the Commanding General of a logistics command and as the Deputy Commanding General of the Theater Support Command during Operation Iraqi Freedom (OIF). Following his tour of duty in the combat zone, he was assigned as the Deputy Commanding General and Chief of Staff, United States Army Reserve in Washington, D.C. His last assignment prior to his retirement was as the Deputy Director (IMA), Office of Business Transformation (Office of the Secretary of the Army).

Dr. Thurgood serves on numerous not-for-profit boards. In 2016, he ran for a U.S. congressional seat.

Dr. Thurgood holds a BA in Political Science from Brigham Young University, an MS in Strategic Studies from the Army War College, an MS in Business Administration from Boston University and a PhD in Organizational Management and Leadership from Capella University. He is a frequent nationally recognized speaker on topics of leadership and operations management.

CPSIA information can be obtained
at www.ICGtesting.com
Printed in the USA
JSHW032312020621
15469JS00002B/13